Mental Toughness Training for Sports

MENTAL
TOUGHNESS
TRAINING FOR
SPORTS
Achieving Athletic Excellence

JAMES E. LOEHR, ED.D.

A PLUME BOOK

PLUME
Published by the Penguin Group
Penguin Books USA Inc., 375 Hudson Street, New York, New York
10014, U.S.A.
Penguin Books Ltd, 27 Wrights Lane, London W8 5TZ, England
Penguin Books Australia Ltd, Ringwood, Victoria, Australia
Penguin Books Canada Ltd, 10 Alcorn Avenue, Toronto, Ontario,
Canada, M4V 3B2
Penguin Books (N.Z.) Ltd, 182-190 Wairau Road, Auckland 10, New
Zealand

Penguin Books Ltd, Registered Offices:
Harmondsworth, Middlesex, England

Published by Plume, an imprint of New American Library, a division
of Penguin Books USA Inc. Previously published in a Stephen Greene
Press Books edition.

First published in 1982 by Forum Publishing Company under the title
Athletic Excellence: Mental Toughness Training for Sports.

10 9 8 7 6 5 4 3

PHOTO CREDITS:

Wide World Photos, Inc.: p. 13 (Jimmy Connors), p. 29 (Billie Jean
King), p. 41 (Tracy Caulkins), p. 63 (Merlin Olsen), p. 68 (Joan
Benoit), p. 88 (Mary Lou Retton), p. 97 (Nancy Lopez), p. 101 (Mary
Decker), p. 107 (Jack Nicklaus), p. 122 (Rick Mears), p. 127 (Bruce
Lee), p. 137 (Nolan Ryan), p. 141 (Bruce Jenner), p. 148 (Larry Bird).
UPI/Bettman Newsphoto: p. 33 (O.J. Simpson), p. 35 (Muhammad
Ali), p. 37 (Pete Rose), p. 49 (U.S. Olympic Hockey Team), p. 78
(Wayne Gretzky), p. 189 (soccer winner). **Joan Russell/Team Russell
Courtesy Head Racquet Sports:** p. 160 (Tim Mayotte). **Head Racquet
Sports:** p. 21 (Tom Gullikson), 23 (Tim Gullikson). Photo on p. 117
courtesy Bill Rodgers. Photo on p. 153 courtesy Jim Plunkett.

Printed in the United States of America
Set in Caledonia
Design by Amy Lamb

*For my father who, with gentle
understanding and patience,
never stopped believing . . .*

"At the peak of tremendous and victorious effort
. . . while the blood is pounding in your head, all
suddenly becomes quiet within you. Everything
seems clearer and whiter than ever before, as if
great spotlights had been turned on. At that moment you have the conviction that you contain all
the power in the world, that you are capable of
everything, that you have wings. There is no more
precious moment in life than this, the white moment, and you will work very hard for years just to
taste it again."[1]

—YURI VLASON
Russian Weight lifter

FOREWORD

D uring my 1975 Wimbledon finals match with Jimmy Connors, I was occasionally seen with my eyes closed when resting between games. This prompted the post-match inquiry, "Were you meditating?" My answer was always "yes and no." "Yes" in the sense that it was a formalized technique of mental and physical relaxation. "No" in that I was not reciting any special words or mantras to myself for ninety seconds. I had simply come to believe at age 33 that I performed better when I was physically conditioned, had a firm game plan in mind, was totally focused on the encounter itself, and remained in control of my actions.

This notion of self-control became an integral part of my tennis training at the very beginning—but for an unusual reason. As part of the first group of Black youngsters in the South to aspire to tennis greatness, I was warned that my future participation depended largely on my ability to exercise an extraordinary degree of self-control. Some tournament directors in the 1950's, it was thought, would use any excuse to deny me entry. My decorum, therefore, had to be beyond reproach.

My tennis mentor, Dr. R. Walter Johnson, thus had a sign posted on the wall for all to see: THOSE WHOM THE GODS WISH TO DESTROY THEY FIRST MAKE MAD. I looked at that sign for eight summers. If at first I followed its dictates because I was told to do so, I soon became a true believer, for dozens of parents of my junior opponents approached Dr. Johnson and marvelled at his students' self-control.

I began to see for myself what my nonplussed game face did to my opponents when matters became tense. I displayed little or no emotion, no matter what the score. The other guy was frequently throwing his racket, cursing, and unravelling. Long past the time when I feared racial resentment, I continued to adopt my nonplussed game face during matches. Not only did it continue to rattle the opposition, it enabled me to minimize the time lost trying to contain nonproductive frustration.

I began to see a heightened interest in this mental side of sport in the early sixties. Television closeups brought the strain of world class competition into our living rooms, and the fan saw a very wide range of human emotions. Doug Sanders missed an eight-inch putt that cost him the British Open. Weight lifters went through psyching rituals that were associated with mental patients. Tommy Bolt threw his golf clubs. Muhammad Ali's pre-fight weigh-ins became case studies for psychiatry students. But one man became a cult figure and the paragon of what the mind can do to enhance athletic performance: Bruce Lee.

The Chinese-born Lee fascinated westerners with his martial arts prowess. His movie, *Enter the Dragon,* captivated audiences and, despite Hollywood special effects, graphically showed the power of the totally focused mind. Professional athletes such as Kareem Abdul-Jabbar became disciples. By the late sixties, owners of professional teams hired consultants to help their players through slumps and to improve performance. In the early seventies, amateur and professional athletes began enrolling in courses designed to improve concentration. Transcendental Meditation, or TM, and est sessions became very popular.

The place of mental discipline in sports has continued to evolve, and now in the eighties, we finally have a manual that details the "whys and hows" of putting the full powers of the mind to work in athletic competition. Jim Loehr has, in essence, crystallized in plain English the recent contributions of Eastern influences on standard Western practices. Though his emphasis pertains to athletics, it becomes obvious to the reader in Chapter I that his advice has relevance to ordinary life as well.

Loehr demystifies certain mental states that lead to athletic success. He makes it clear that, given the raw talent, the mental and emotional control needed to extract that nth degree of performance is a *learned,* not inborn, trait. The professional athletes, who in Western Civilization are rewarded in ways that only rock stars can appreciate, have learned mental discipline. These sports superstars who sometimes personify our fantasies of physical prowess or grace, have mastered lessons that everyone can learn.

Loehr's lessons apply to athletes of all age groups and performance levels and can serve as a primer for coaches and administrators. Young teenaged athletes, for example, cannot help but be influenced by our instant-gratification society in this Age of Entitlement. Team sports offer excellent antidotes for some of these recent distorted notions of self. It was no accident that the seventies was known as the "me decade." The stretched out periods of training required for consistent team success clearly belie the belief among some of our nation's children that success comes overnight.

Young adults will quickly see parallels between their own occupational stresses and what Loehr calls his Ideal Performance State for athletes. The copy writer who occasionally experiences periods of heightened creative expression and the production manager who, every once in a while, orchestrates all his labor and materials in perfect synchronization are working from this state. This state of mind—when all the positive elements converge at once to produce "superhuman" results—is what athletes and teams strive for. But the results were not superhuman after all. The potential was always there, waiting for someone to put the pieces together.

There are many examples of extraordinary feats in sports. The single most impressive feat, I believe, was Bob Beamon's record long jump at the Mexico City Olympics in 1968. Beamon was in his Ideal Performance State and broke the world record by almost two feet. No one has come close since.

There have been other examples of athletes who have "put it together" when the pressure was on and made it look easy. Julius Erving, John McEnroe, O. J. Simpson, Muhammad Ali, Willie Mays, Billie Jean King, Joanne Carner, the Pittsburgh Steelers, the Boston Celtics, the New York Yankees, John Wooden, and Red Auerbach are examples of players, teams, and coaches who were able to reach and maintain athletic excellence.

Jim Loehr has fashioned a treatise that is literally "athletic food for thought." Read it. Study it. Try it. *Do it.*

—ARTHUR ASHE

CONTENTS

MENTAL
TOUGHNESS
TRAINING FOR
SPORTS

INTRODUCTION

This book is about mental toughness. Most of us as athletes understand how to train physically. We know how to work to improve our fitness, strength, and physical skills. But how do we train to become better competitors, to improve our mental toughness? Most coaches and athletes agree that at least 50 percent of the process of playing well is mental. If you are like most athletes, however, you rarely spend 5 percent of your total training time refining your mental skills. The obvious question is *why*? If we as coaches and athletes acknowledge the critical importance of the mental factor, why don't we train for it? The answer is that we do not know how to train. The whole area of mental training can seem confusing, hopelessly complex, and even at times self-contradictory. The Athletic Excellence Training (AET) system fills that void.

Chapter I provides important background information regarding sport psychology and the origin of AET. It also addresses the ultimate measure of mental toughness in an athlete and describes the toughest opponent a performing athlete will ever face.

Chapter II establishes the vital connection between mental toughness and control of a very specific constellation of feelings referred to as the Ideal Performance State (IPS). The role our emotions play in peak performance as well as which emotions are most critical to competitive success are addressed in this chapter. The connection between mental toughness and a specific kind of energy, thinking style, and mental focus is also explained here.

The primary AET procedures for accelerating Ideal Performance State Control are the core of Chapter III. As pointed out in this chapter, IPS control and competitive success are nearly synonymous.

Special areas of mental training that should be used to augment and further refine IPS control are provided in Chapter IV. Topics include visualization, self-motivation, muscle relaxation, managing negative energy, meditation, breath control, activation, and centering. Also covered are strategies for dealing with performance slumps, preparation routines for competition, and becoming a team player.

Chapter V provides a tool for assessing one's mental toughness skills as well as tools for monitoring a variety of physical performance factors potentially descriptive of one's mood control during competition. A list of recommended readings is also provided.

THE ULTIMATE CHALLENGE

Athletic competition contains much of the drama of life—in many respects, it is a microcosm of life. Frustration, joy, uncertainty, pain, and struggle are all there. People who enter the competitive arena soon realize that there is more to competition than simply learning the physical skills. It is one thing to possess the physical skills and yet another to be able to use them when it counts. And therein lies the challenge—the ultimate challenge of self-control. In the final analysis, every athletic contest is a contest of control, control of the delicate mind-body connection. The link between our minds and our bodies is dramatically clear within the competitive arena.

To perform toward the upper limits of our physical skill and talent when we most want to do that often seems beyond us. This struggle brings us face to face with ourselves, our insecurities, our doubts, our inadequacies, and our fears. Success in competition demands that we move beyond this struggle into mastery of ourselves. The mastering of competitive sport, then, becomes a continuous process of self-transformation, change, and rebirth. Such mastery involves courage, commitment, and discipline. In short, it is a contest of each person against himself.

Just as physical fitness and strength are central to competitive performance, so also is mental fitness. Consistently performing to your peak in the heat of competitive battle requires *mental strength*, a strength that is fundamentally embodied in a core of *acquired* mental skills. Those skills include concentrating, controlling attitude, managing pressure, thinking right, controlling energy, staying motivated, and visualizing. And that's what Athletic Excellence Training is all about: meeting the ultimate challenge and building mental strength. It's about excellence, joy, fulfillment, and struggle. It's also a step-by-step procedure for understanding and controlling that indefinable but critical mind-body connection. Controlling this connection is the essence of MENTAL TOUGHNESS in sport, and Athletic Excellence Training is designed to brighten and shorten that process.

A PERSONAL JOURNEY

The journey into mental toughness, a seemingly subtle and intangible journey, is captured in the following passage.

The game is about to begin. In less than an hour, I'm going to be put to the test. All of my training, hard work, and effort are suddenly past. There is only now.

Somehow, though, things are different this time. The new learnings and understandings have changed me. I'm still a little shaky inside, my palms are wet, and I am a little nervous. That's the same, but there are differences. I'm looking forward to performing in a way I never have before. I feel like a kid again—I'm excited. I feel lucky to have the chance to do what I'm about to do. I've never felt that way. In the past I've always felt a crazy combination of obligation, expectation, commitment, and fear.

Oh, I can't say it was never fun or that I never looked forward to it. But it wasn't the same as now. Before I was too busy trying to perform well to enjoy myself. I was too busy trying not to look stupid or trying to break some new record. If I broke the record, I was extremely happy. If I looked and performed lousy, I was miserable. During the performance, I always got caught up in which it would be—a new record or another catastrophe. I hated losing. That hasn't changed, but the focus has.

I'm not playing "not to lose" anymore. I still want to perform to my best, to break that new record, to walk away victorious, but something important has changed. My focus now is the MOMENT. After much convincing and experimentation, I finally put into practice something that has transformed me into a performer. The outcome is as much a surprise to me as it is to everyone else—I can perform! And the changes in myself that are responsible for the transformation seem subtle and insignificant; the changes are almost too simple to put into words.

I have learned to focus on the MOMENT. I *savor* the moment. Every moment of every performance is something to be fully experienced and enjoyed. I take each moment for what it is, and whenever I do that, I immediately experience a sense of calm, strength, and energy. I seem to glow inside.

When I savor the moment, a new and powerful source of energy gets released within me. I immediately feel more positive and more in control. Things start flowing automatically. There's no tension, no anxiety, no fear. As soon as I lose this moment, however, as soon as I start thinking about winning and losing, what I should have done or what could happen, all the negatives come charging back.

I had been told and had read many times that I should perform in the present, but it didn't make any sense to me. It seemed like so much philosophy—not related to my everyday trials. I'm a jock (whatever that means), and I resist intellectual and philosophical verbiage. I like action, doing things, getting the job done. As soon as living in the moment became real for me, my performance began to change dramatically for the better.

The one basic understanding that made the difference is that I perform best when I savor the moment, when I am right here and now and love every minute of it. As long as what I'm physically doing at that moment is what I am mentally doing at that moment, everything happens naturally. I don't have to *try* to get psyched or *try* to concentrate or *try* to perform well. I just do. And when I'm there, I've got excess energy, and I'm mentally on target. My mind and body seem to click. I'm no longer fighting against myself. I understand what is meant by flowing *with* the current rather than against it.

The price I paid to reach this point has been high. I wonder if it was all that necessary. As I reflect back on the years of struggle, the frustrations, the doubt, the self-condemnation, the agony of knowing what I could do against what I did do, I feel a genuine sadness. Jock or not, my eyes begin to swell as I relive the years. The price was great. Why was it so hard? What made the whole thing so damned difficult?

The answer is painfully clear—*I* did! I kept getting in the way. I was bound and determined to succeed, and I wanted to win at all costs. Nothing would stand in my way. I wanted to prove to myself and to everyone else that I could do it. My answer was simple: *try harder* and *be stronger*. No one ever told me that trying *softer*, not harder, might be the key, or that inner calmness would bring strength. The anger, frustration, agony, and disappointment were not so much from losing as from knowing that I performed considerably below what I was capable of doing. When I wanted it most, I was incapable of performing well. And the reason is now clear—I tried *too* hard; I was forcing it.

Performing well, I've learned, occurs naturally or it doesn't occur at all. For me, *trying* to play better, *trying* not to get angry, *trying* to concentrate, or *trying* not to be nervous made the situation worse. I was fighting the current rather than going with it. I've learned there's a difference between trying harder and giving 100 percent effort. I still give 100 percent effort, and I still don't like losing, but there is something distinctively different—I don't get in the way as much anymore.

I used to worry about the guy on the other side. I understand now that it's me, not him, that I should be concerned with. By comparison, he's easy. I've always been my own toughest opponent, and I suppose I always will be. The odds are much better now, though. Savoring the moment gives me a handle. It does two things: it brings me back to doing what I'm doing, and it suddenly makes it fun again. Playing my best always seems to happen when I'm feeling a particular way. I feel pumped-up, positive, confident, and invincible. Keeping those feelings for any length of time used to be a problem. Something would happen, even something little, and suddenly they would be gone. All that was left was to try harder, so I did. When I stay with the moment, the feelings are much easier to keep, and when I lose them, I can get them back in the same way.

Don't misunderstand. The feelings don't *always* come, and I still lose them sometimes and can't get them back. I'm still my own toughest opponent, but I'm winning that contest most of the time now. And sometimes the feelings don't come. Even when I go to the moment, they can be a little stubborn. To help them along, I'll start acting "as if" they were there. Often that's enough to get the feelings going again. As soon as that happens, I start becoming a performer again.

I used to think those feelings came only when I played well. I had it backwards. I played well because I got the feelings, and there's a big difference. When I feel right, I perform right, and when I don't, I don't—no matter how hard I try. The right feelings come when I live in every moment, when I love and savor every moment—when I am in the NOW.

I don't know how or why I stayed in sports for as long as I did. I nearly called it quits a hundred times. Whatever it was, I'm thankful because it's been a real personal triumph, a triumph that has made the payoff worth much more than the price. I suppose the price was necessary for me, but that was only because I didn't understand. If only I could get others to understand, but . . . Would it all seem like just so many meaningless words as it did to me? Maybe not . . .

CHAPTER I
MENTAL
TOUGHNESS

THE LAST FRONTIER OF SPORT

The advances we've made in the science of sport over the past twenty years have been remarkable. We have become highly sophisticated in physical fitness, nutrition, biomechanics, and human physiology as they relate to athletic performance. We can design and implement very precise training programs that lead directly to desired changes in aerobic capacity, form and technique, strength and flexibility, weight, body fat, and other performance factors. The recent resurgence of interest in sports medicine in this country is leading to significant advances in the management, prevention, and rehabilitation of sport-related injuries. We are quickly closing the knowledge gap in these areas.

But what about the mental side of sport? How important is it, and what can be done to systematically improve an athlete's mental toughness if it *is* important? For nearly two and one-half years I conducted interviews with top athletes and coaches from the United States, Canada, and Japan, where these questions were asked. By their own admission, athletes and coaches contend that at least 50 percent of the process of playing well is the result of mental or psychological factors. Many felt that the process of performing well was 70 to 90 percent mental. When asked, however, how much of their total practice time they devoted to strengthening these mental skills, they reported between five and ten percent maximum. If the mental skills, by their own admission, represent at least fifty percent of the process, why do coaches and athletes spend only five to ten percent of their time working on these skills? The answer: they don't know what or how to practice. There has been no available psychological training model that they could follow.

In the United States, the field of sport psychology has substantially grown since the latter 1960's. By comparison, however, sport psychology lags far behind most other sport-related sciences; it is still in its infancy. The slow growth of the field is not due to lack of interest or commitment. The problem has been in dealing with its complexity, for the dimension and scope of the human mind can be quickly overwhelming. Employing the same scientific procedures that are useful in most other sciences presents staggering problems to researchers intent on carving out new understandings and knowledge concerning the mind and its relation to sports.

Describing the dilemma well, my former psychology professor began his course on research methods in psychology by writing on the board:

> *"The mind, in attempting to understand itself, is faced with the situation in which the object to be understood (namely, the human mind) and that which must understand (the mind) are of equal complexity."*

The challenge of the 1980's and 1990's will be to successfully unlock the door to this last frontier of sport. In fact, I predict that the dominant theme in sport during this period will be understanding, teaching, and controlling the dimensions of mental toughness.

The AET model presented here is one step in that process.

No One Ever Told Me!

For many years I thought I was different. I was convinced there was a missing link inside me. I knew what I could do as an athlete, but I was never able to put it together when it counted. I loved the game but I hated myself. Why couldn't I successfully compete? What was the matter with me? As a young player, I was overwhelmed by frustration, anger, and self-doubt. I vowed to give up the game scores of times. As I look back, I can see that I fought myself every inch of the way.

During competition, my inner world was a frantic mixture of panic and rage. The panic was tied to a seemingly endless line-up of fears— fear of looking bad, fear of losing to someone I shouldn't, fear of choking, fear of winning, and on and on. The rage reflected frustration and disappointment with myself. These emotions would build inside me until I thought I would burst. And the result was always the same—mistake after mistake and failure after failure. The only answer I knew was to try harder. If you had asked me at the time if my muscles got tight or my head fast and frantic, I surely would have responded with a quick "no."

Relaxation, calmness, and quiet had no meaning to me as a competitor. But then, no one ever told me they were important. According to my coaches, mastering the fundamentals and good solid conditioning were the answers. And that's what I stayed with year after year, tournament after tournament. I was nearly thirty years old before I learned that there was an easier way. That "easier way" is what I call Athletic Excellence Training (AET).

MENTAL TOUGHNESS AND CONSISTENCY

Why do you play well one day and poorly the next? Athletes often feel like they're on a performance roller coaster—one day up and one day down, one moment on top and the next at the bottom. As one competitor put it, "I feel like I'm playing Russian Roulette with myself every time I perform. When I walk onto the athletic field, I never know whether I'll play poorly and get blown away or play well and be spared. It all seems strangely out of my control."

There are few things more frustrating in sport than knowing full well that you rarely play to your potential when it counts. This dilemma can be a powerful trigger of guilt, self-doubt, anger, and self-criticism. Every serious competitor hits this intangible barrier more than once, and some never get beyond it. When that happens, people start dropping out, because the price is too great—the frustration and mental anguish are not worth the triumphs. Those who fail to move beyond this impasse are the casualties of competitive sport. Young developing athletes are particularly prone to this misfortune, but it occurs with all skill levels and age groups.

How do you achieve consistency in performance? What is the process or learning that allows you to begin performing consistently to your potential? Reaching and performing at potential is the focus of all mental training. Not surprisingly, consistency is the ultimate measure of mental toughness in an athlete; it is also the earmark of a champion.

Performing toward the upper range of your talent and skill day after day and year after year requires two things. The first is good technique and form. Much inconsistency in sport is the result of poor biomechanics. If your technique is poor, no matter how mentally tough you are, performance inconsistencies will persist.

The second element for consistency in performance is good mental skills. The mentally tough competitor is consistent in performance precisely because he is consistent psychologically. Ups and downs in performance are often directly traceable to psychological ups and downs. As you will see, playing well is the result of creating a particular atmosphere within yourself. Put very simply, players who can consistently create this special atmosphere or climate within themselves perform consistently.

Setting the Record Straight

I want to set the record straight. No matter what you've heard, where you've heard it, or who you've heard it from, the simple fact is: MENTAL TOUGHNESS IS LEARNED, NOT INHERITED. Granted, we digest our failures more easily if we believe that we were born into the world sadly lacking some critical mental toughness gene or instinct. That's a very tempting position because, if we don't make it, we are absolved of all responsibility. As one very talented but highly frustrated athlete put it just before retiring from competitive play, "I realize I have all the talent and skill, but unfortunately, I was not born with the necessary competitive instincts."

General personality style is also unrelated to mental toughness. Whether you're an introvert or extrovert, quiet or boastful, dynamic or reserved, has little bearing on your success as a competitor. You need not move out of your own normal and comfortable personality style to achieve a high degree of mental toughness.

There is, however, a constellation of mental skills, *all of which are learned*, that are characteristic of mentally tough competitors. They are:

- **Self-Motivated and Self-Directed.**
  He doesn't need to be pushed, shoved, or forced from the outside. His direction comes from within. He's involved because he wants to be, because it's his thing, not somebody else's.
- **Positive but Realistic.**
  He's not a complainer, a criticizer, or a faultfinder. He's a builder, not a destroyer. His trademark is a blend of realism and optimism. His eye is always fixed on success, on what *can* happen, and on what is possible—not on their opposites.
- **In Control of His Emotions.**
  Every player or competitor understands all too well the unfortunate performance consequences of poor emotional control. Bad refereeing, stupid mistakes, obnoxious opponents, poor playing conditions, etc., represent powerful triggers of negative emotion. Anger, frustration, and fear must be controlled, or they most certainly will control you. The tough competitor has tamed the lion inside.
- **Calm and Relaxed Under Fire.**
  He doesn't avoid pressure; he's challenged by it. He's at his best when the pressure is on and the odds are against him. Being put to the test is not a threat. It's another opportunity to explore the outer limits of his potential.
- **Highly Energetic and Ready for Action.**
  He is capable of getting himself pumped up and energized for playing his best, no matter how he feels or how bad or meaningless the situation. He is his own igniter and can do so in spite of fatigue, personal problems, or bad luck.
- **Determined.**
  His sheer force of will to succeed in what he has started is beyond comprehension for those who do not share the same vision. He is relentless in his pursuit of his goals. Setbacks are taken in stride as he inches his way further forward.

- **Mentally Alert and Focused.**
  He is capable of long and intensive periods of total concentration. He is capable of tuning in what's important and tuning out what's not, whether there is no pressure or great pressure. In short, he has attentional control.
- **Doggedly Self-Confident.**
  He displays a nearly unshatterable sense of confidence and belief in himself and in his ability to perform well. He rarely falls victim to his own or others' self-defeating thoughts and ideas. As a consequence, he is not easily intimidated. On the contrary, because of his confident appearance, he often becomes the intimidator.
- **Fully Responsible.**
  He takes full responsibility for his own actions. There are no excuses. He either did or he didn't. Ultimately, everything begins and ends with him, and he is comfortable with that. He is fully aware that his destiny as an athlete is in his own hands. His future is his own.

The athletes who fit this description best dominate the world of sports. The world's greatest athletes give testimony to the reality of mental toughness every time they perform. All the great artists of sport have exemplified this special kind of inner strength, a strength that goes well beyond the limits of their natural talent and skill. It is the thin line which separates the few who make it from the thousands who don't. The deciding factor is always the same: your INNER STRENGTH makes the ultimate difference.

THE CONTEST WITH YOURSELF

The Ultimate Battle

The world's top athletes almost universally agree on one thing: *You will always be your own toughest opponent.*

Until you can conquer *yourself*, very little is possible against an opponent. The greatest obstacle between you and your goal is *YOU!* Once you have learned to control you, the contest with the outside world or your noble opponent becomes easy. Experience has shown

Jimmy Connors is one of the mentally toughest athletes of all time. His relentless will to fight has shaped his destiny in a most powerful way. He believes that winning is at least 95 percent mental.

that to perform at your best, you should have one focus: *doing the best that you can.*

Focusing on winning and losing the external contest too frequently leads to performance paralysis. Fears of winning and losing quickly lead to muscle tightness, excessive anxiety, and poor concentration. Focusing on "doing the very best you can" and on "winning the contest with yourself" rarely leads to such performance problems.

Here's how to win the match with yourself. If you can answer "yes" to each of the following three statements at the end of play or practice, you have won the most important contest.

1. I gave my best effort every moment. I gave 100 percent.
2. I maintained a predominantly positive, healthy, and optimistic attitude with myself.
3. I accepted full responsibility for me today, for what I did and didn't do (didn't blame parents, weather, bad equipment, cheating opponent, or anything else).

Winning the contest with yourself is hard work—it is the *ultimate challenge.* You must realize, however, that you *can* succeed with yourself every day. This is precisely how you build success, the most satisfying and fulfilling of all—the conquest of self. You will be victorious with your opponents more frequently than your physical talents and skill should allow when you consistently win the inner contest. This area of learning becomes the foundation of *MENTAL STRENGTH.*

The following passage, written by a runner in response to the question "Why do I run?" captures the essence of self-challenge.

> *Why do I run?*
> *Those who don't can't understand.*
> *The pain is real every day.*
> *Is it easier now? Not really—*
> *The same pain I felt the first day*
> *   I began.*
> *Only easier to cover greater*
> *   distances in shorter periods of time.*
> *The pain is the same, and I understand*
> *   it always will be.*
> *I dread it, and in a sense I crave it.*
> *Why do I run?*
> *To stay in shape, to keep my health,*

To feel better—all partial reasons,
   I suppose.
The real reason is confirmation—confirmation
   that I am in control.
Every day I must make a choice—a choice
   to experience pain and discomfort in order
   to achieve a higher goal or to give in to
   the body's urging to do something else more
   comforting and pleasurable.
Who is in control? My body or me?
Every time I run, I verify to me that
   I am in control and that I can be the
   master of my own destiny.
That is ultimately why I run.
I feel guilty when I don't run—
   when the body wins
Running is a test of my strength—
   not just my physical—but my mental.
Running is a challenge of my "will"—
   of mind over matter, of me
   against myself.
Running is mental conditioning as well
   as physical.
It's therapy of the "will" for me.
Each run is success—the richest and
   most deeply satisfying.
Strangely but unmistakenly tied to self-
   discipline, self-denial and self-control.
In a world where I often feel helpless,
   victimized and controlled, running
   helps revive feelings of hope, strength,
   and conviction that
     I can make a difference
      and
     I can be responsible for me.
An addiction or choice, you say.
   And you're right—there's a danger.
So long as I "choose," the value remains
   true and real;
So long as I control running and not
   running—me.
Positive addiction or not, the value
   is in choosing.

When the choice is gone, I become
controlled and victimized again,
One more thing in my life that tells me
I am not in control, that
I am simply a pawn of fate and circumstance.
I must run as a choice, not out of necessity
or its real value again is gone for me.
Why do I run?
I run for success, success in the
ultimate contest.
The contest of me against myself.

A Formula for Success

The following four-step formula evolved from interviews and discussions with top performing athletes conducted over a period of nearly ten years. Presented here as a first look, it will take on greater meaning for you as the training progresses.

- STEP 1: self-discipline. Everything worthwhile begins at this level. It simply means doing whatever you have to do and making whatever sacrifices are necessary to get the job done the best you know how. It's hard work; it's giving up things you like in order to achieve a higher goal.
- STEP 2: self-control. Self-discipline leads directly to self-control. As you discipline yourself, you experience steady increases in self-control—control of what you do, what you think, and how you react. Without self-control, being the best you can be as an athlete is nothing more than a fantasy.
- STEP 3: self-confidence. Self-control leads directly to self-confidence. What tracks are to a train, self-confidence is to the athlete—without it, he can go nowhere. Self-confidence, that unshatterable belief in yourself, comes from knowing that you are in control.
- STEP 4: self-realization. Self-realization is simply becoming the best you can be, the manifestation of your talent and skill as an athlete. It is the fulfillment and the ecstasy of sport. Self-realization follows di-

rectly from self-confidence. Once you believe in *yourself* and feel good about yourself, you are opening doors to your fullest potential.

Spend some time thinking about this simple formula. Think about how it relates to you within the realm of sport as well as outside it.

> *"Success is peace of mind, which is a direct result of self-satisfaction in knowing you did your best to become the best that you are capable of becoming."*
> —John Wooden
> One of the winningest basketball coaches in history.

THE AET MODEL

The Foundation

The following summary statements represent the basic foundation of the Athletic Excellence Training program.

- *Mental toughness is learned, not inherited.*
   This is an important understanding. Very simply, if you are a mentally tough competitor, you *learned* to be one, and if you're not, you didn't. Mental toughness has nothing to do with your heredity, your intelligence, or your character—mental toughness is an *acquired* skill. The process through which it is acquired is precisely the same as that which applies to physical skills—hard work, understanding, and practice. The point is this: if you want to be mentally tougher, you can!
- *The ultimate measure of mental toughness is consistency.*
   From Bjorn Borg to Jerry West and from Phil Esposito to Jack Nicklaus, one element is always the same—a remarkable level of performance consistency. Athletes such as these daily demonstrate that they have acquired something

very special. They have gained a high degree of control over the process of playing toward the upper range of their capabilities. The distinguishing trademark of players such as these is not so much the exceptional talent, but rather their exceptional ability to consistently play to the peak of their talent.

The ultimate test of the AET model is the extent to which it leads to increased performance consistency.

CHAPTER II
THE AET MODEL

THE ORIGIN OF AET

I wish I could claim that the Athletic Excellence Training model presented here is exclusively my conception. It is not. Much of it is the strategy for success as conceived, experienced, and lived by hundreds of successful athletes and coaches. This model represents their story, their struggle for answers, and their path to personal triumph. My contribution has been to listen and to learn from their building blocks of success. I have been synthesizer and integrator, interpreter and model builder, using their experience as both fabric and foundation.

Obviously, my experience as a professional psychologist, professional athlete, and coach have helped immeasurably with the process. Scientific writings and formalized research into the field of sport psychology, as well as my own personal research in the field, have also been important to the effort. I am convinced, however, that the success of the AET model for both players and coaches is largely due to the fact that it comes from the players and coaches themselves. It is not another sport psychology "armchair theory." It makes sense and gets results precisely because it rests firmly on the experience of performing athletes themselves.

As new understanding and learning emerge, new techniques will be added, some will be discarded, and many others will take a new form. The basic foundation and model, however, will most likely persist for some time, for it is firmly rooted in the wisdom of collective experience. The performing athlete himself is both the question and the answer.

- *Excepting the influence of physical factors, performance consistency is the result of psychological consistency.*

  Consistency on the outside requires consistency on the inside. Athletes who typically find themselves on a psychological roller coaster rarely experience performance consistency. Psychological control is a prerequisite for performance control. The ability to establish and maintain a stable internal climate during competitive play has proved to be one of the most important factors in competitive success.

- *The extent to which individuals or teams will perform toward the upper range of their talent and skill largely depends on the success they have in creating and maintaining a particular kind of mental climate within themselves.*

  Comparing the performance ups and downs of competitive athletes during play with changes that occur psychologically gives us critical understanding. When athletes are performing well, they invariably are experiencing a *highly distinct and specific mental state*. Over and over again the results were the same. And the opposite was also true. To the extent that an athlete was unable to establish this particular mental state, performance levels suffered.

- *Excepting the influence of physical factors, the level of performance of individuals or teams is an accurate reflection of the kind of internal climate existing within the performers themselves.*

  Peak performance occurs naturally when the right internal conditions are present. Playing well or playing poorly is a natural reflection of the mental state that you are experiencing at the time. When the right internal conditions are present, playing toward the upper range of your capabilities occurs automatically.

Tom Gullikson went from his worst year as a pro to his all-time best in terms of both world ranking and tournament earnings after he began the AET program. At the age of thirty-four, he feels he is playing the best tennis of his career. "Mental Toughness was the difference."

- *An ideal internal performance climate exists for every athlete and every team. This is referred to as the Ideal Performance State.*

  Most athletes are only vaguely aware of the existence of such a state. Few have made the connection between the occurrence of this state and playing well. Although top competitors have achieved a high degree of control over this state, the control is largely unconscious.

- *The component elements of the Ideal Performance State are fundamentally the same for all athletes and across all sports.*

  This was perhaps the most surprising and most significant finding of all. Athletes consistently chose to describe their inner psychological states during peak performance periods in the same way. As performance levels dropped, their descriptions of simultaneous psychological changes followed the same patterns.

- *The Ideal Performance State is most accurately described in terms of specific feeling states experienced by the individual performers.*

  As we currently have no concrete way to directly monitor and measure an athlete's internal states during play, the most effective alternative thus far has been to monitor ongoing feeling states. As biofeedback instrumentation becomes more sophisticated and portable, a more direct and precise form of measurement will eventually be possible. In actuality, the technology is nearly complete now. The ability to scientifically monitor an athlete's internal states and physiological arousal levels during play will add an exciting dimension in precision and understanding.

- *The most important mental skills required in competitive sport are those associated with creating and maintaining the Ideal Performance State during play.*

  Controlling the Ideal Performance State is directly related to the acquisition of a core of essential mental skills. These skills are the direct focus of the Athletic Excellence Training procedures.

- *Mental toughness requires a high degree of control over the Ideal Performance State. The more you practice, the better you get.*

Tim Gullikson went from a world ranking of 150 to 32nd within six months of starting the AET program. "I learned how to become less analytical and more instinctive and automatic during play."

Maintaining the right internal climate when things are going your way is tough enough. The real test of your mental skill comes, however, when the pressure is on, when the world is against you, and when everything has turned upside down. Then you face the limits of your mental strength.

THE IDEAL PERFORMANCE STATE

The single most important concept within the AET model is the Ideal Performance State. This concept first emerged as the observation that athletes consistently choose similar words and phrases to describe their inner experience when they perform well. That observation eventually led to the formulation of a promising hypothesis:

> *A measurably different mental or psychological state exists when an athlete is performing well, as opposed to when he/she is performing poorly.*

This hypothesis appeared promising because it addressed the fundamental issue of consistency. As pointed out earlier, performance inconsistency can stem from a variety of physical factors, such as poor technique, fatigue, physical injuries, and so on. But, all too often, performance inconsistencies seem clearly unrelated to such physical factors. When this is the case, a different set of answers must be found, answers that are psychological, not physical. From a psychological perspective, then, why do athletes perform well one month or day and poorly the next? Something psychological must be changing; a more precise look shows that many of the agonizing ups and downs so often experienced by performing athletes may be directly traceable to psychological changes.

Testing the Hypothesis

The first step taken in the search for answers was to systematically collect information from performing athletes relative to their internal feeling states during play. Athletes were first asked to rate the level of their play immediately following a performance. They were then asked to describe in writing and in as much detail as possible what their internal psychological experience was like during the performance. The initial sample consisted of forty-three professional and amateur athletes from a total of seven different sports. The sample was eventually extended to include over three hundred performers.

The second step was to have performing athletes recall from memory their "finest hour" as a player and then describe in writing what their internal psychological experience was like during that performance. They were then to do exactly the same thing for their "worst hour."

Once the material had been collected, correlations were made between the words the athletes used to describe their internal experience and whether the performance was, in their judgment, a good or bad one.

The Results

Over and over, the same words consistently appeared when the athletes attempted to describe what was occurring internally when they performed well. The same held true for poor performances.

The following is a composite of the internal climate most commonly experienced by athletes during an outstanding performance.

> *"I felt physically very relaxed, but really energized
> and pumped up. I experienced virtually no anxiety
> or fear, and the whole experience was totally
> enjoyable. I experienced a very real sense of
> calmness and quiet inside, and everything just
> seemed to flow automatically. I really didn't have to
> think about what I was supposed to do; it just
> seemed to happen naturally.*
>
> *"Even though I was really hustling, it was all very
> effortless. I always seemed to have enough time
> and energy and rarely felt rushed—almost at times
> as if I were performing in slow motion. I felt like I
> could do almost anything, as if I were in complete
> control. I really felt confident and positive.*
>
> *"It also seemed very easy to concentrate. I was
> totally tuned in to what I was doing. I was also
> super-aware—aware of everything but distracted*

> *by nothing. It almost seemed like I knew what was*
> *going to happen before it actually did."*

As it turned out, this simple description proved indispensable to the task of building an effective mental toughness training program. It led the way to the development of the following critical understandings.

1. Your level of performance is a direct reflection of the way you feel inside.
2. When you feel right, you can perform right.
3. Playing well is a natural consequence of the right kind of internal feelings.
4. Playing as well as you can at the moment occurs *automatically* when the right emotional balance has been established.
5. In the final analysis, mental toughness is the ability to create and maintain the right kind of internal feeling regardless of the circumstances.
6. The most important step you can take to perform to your best is to create a particular climate within yourself and maintain it, *no matter what!*

Which Comes First— The Chicken or the Egg?

The Ideal Performance State (IPS) concept raises an important question. Which comes first—the right inner state or the good performance? Is the IPS simply a consequence of playing well, or is it a cause? The chicken and the egg controversy may never be resolved, but the IPS question can comfortably answered. The mind-body connection that manifests in excelling performance becomes impossible when the wrong internal climate is present. The internal state comes first. When the right internal climate takes form, playing well occurs *naturally* and *spontaneously*.

The right internal climate helps to bridge a gap, the gap between what you *can* do as an athlete and what you *actually do*, between your potential and the realization of that potential. The wrong climate is like trying to get a seed to grow in frozen soil. The climate and conditions just won't allow the seed and soil to properly connect. But as soon as the conditions are right—the right combination of temperature, water, and so on—the connection is easily made, and the potential of one with the other can be realized. So, too, with performance potential. Establishing the right internal climate (Ideal Performance State) leads to the realization of your potential.

A Closer Look at the IPS

From the analysis of several hundred reports of performing athletes, twelve distinct categories emerged, reflecting the ideal internal climate for performing optimally. Twelve aspects of the ideal climate are:

Physically relaxed	Effortless
Mentally calm	Automatic
Low anxiety	Alert
Energized	Mentally focused
Optimistic	Self-confident
Enjoyment	In control

Another way of saying the same thing is that you will perform best when you experience the following feelings:

- When you feel relaxed and loose.
- When you feel a sense of calmness and quiet inside.
- When you feel no anxiety or nervousness.
- When you feel charged with high energy.
- When you feel optimistic and positive.
- When you feel a genuine sense of fun and enjoyment in your play.
- When your performance feels effortless.
- When you feel automatic and spontaneous in your play.
- When you feel mentally alert.
- When you feel mentally focused and tuned in.
- When you feel highly self-confident.
- When you feel in control of yourself.

The entire Athletic Excellence Training system is geared to helping you achieve control over this special mental state. The training procedures and concepts are specifically designed to help you acquire the necessary mental skills that will enable you to identify, trigger, and maintain your own Ideal Performance State, regardless of the circumstances of play.

Because of the central importance of this concept to the entire training program, it is important to fully understand each feeling component. From experience, I know that many performing athletes have considerable misunderstanding as to what must happen psychologically for them to play well. Once you understand what you're trying to achieve with your head, the process suddenly becomes much easier. Let's clear up those misunderstandings.

Physically Relaxed

For years, I thought getting psyched up and ready for play was somehow tied to being a little tight and nervous. I thought that if my muscles didn't feel a little tight, I would play flat, and I didn't want that. To play with intensity, I needed to get emotionally charged up, and my muscles needed to be a little tight. When my research revealed quite the opposite, I was surprised.

Athletes perform best when they're feeling loose, when they're experiencing no nervous muscle tension. The more a sport requires delicate, fine motor skill, the more critical it is that your muscles are completely relaxed and loose. Even in a general sense, athletes do not perform best when their muscles feel moderately or even slightly tight. Top performance occurs when muscles feel loose and free. As we'll see later on, tight muscles and nervousness *before* you play are not necessarily a problem; *during* play they almost always are.

Mentally Calm

This is one of the most important ingredients of the twelve. It is also the most misunderstood. All too often, athletes equate being psyched and pumped for play with a fast, accelerated mental state. The fact is that athletes consistently report that when they are performing well, they are experiencing a sense of calm and quiet inside. The evidence thus far collected also indicates that an athlete's success in concentrating and responding intelligently during play is directly related to pthis calmness. A host of familiar performance problems generally surface when mental calmness is replaced with a racy, fast,

Billie Jean King reports that she performs best when she is able
to take herself beyond the turmoil of the court to a place of complete inner peace and calm.

accelerated mental state. That mental calmness is often accompanied
by the feeling that things are going in slow motion.

> *"Everything seemed to slow down, and I had all the
> time in the world to make my move."*

Low Anxiety

I had always thought that a little anxiety and nervousness were helpful. Even the formal research in this area indicated this, so I was surprised when I learned that athletes perform best when they feel *no anxiety* whatsoever. As soon as athletes began to feel even a little nervous or anxious, their performance levels dropped. The only exception to this was when an athlete could not get energized or pumped to perform from positive sources. In other words, if he was emotionally or motivationally flat, anxiety proved to be a helpful energy source. Even in these cases, however, athletes rarely achieved high levels of performance when anxiety was used as an energy source. You perform best when you are energized from positive sources and simultaneously experience no anxiety or nervousness. In order to be a good performer, you must be able to take tough and difficult situations and make them PRESSURE FREE. The greatness of a Gretzky, a Connors, a Palmer, or an Evert is not that they perform so well *under pressure*. No one performs well under pressure. Their greatness is in their learned ability to take the pressure off.

Energized

Along with calmness, feeling properly energized ranks high in importance. So far, we've got an athlete who is loose, calm and quiet, and experiencing no anxiety. From the description so far, he could be sleeping!

Athletes consistently described their best performances occurring when they felt pumped with energy. The source of the energy was not anxiety, fear, anger, or frustration. On the contrary, the one word that captured the energy source best, as described by the athletes themselves, was *JOY*. Feelings of enjoyment and fun and loving what they were doing were strongly tied to the right energy source. The reports of the athletes point to the need for differentiating between positive and negative sources of energy. Performing well is fundamentally linked to the presence of *positive* energy.

Another important understanding is that, according to the athletes themselves, you can never get too much positive energy. "The more, the better—the more joy, the more fun, the more you love what you're doing, the better." As we'll see later, this finding seemed to directly contradict previous research findings and was initially very puzzling. The experience of the athletes, however, proved to be correct. Performing toward the peak of one's talent and skill is clearly related to high levels of positive energy accompanied by a profound sense of inner calmness, a unique and intriguing combination.

Optimistic

The importance of feeling positive and optimistic to performing well is no myth. If there's any doubt in your mind, start asking successful athletes how they feel about it, and you'll quickly be convinced. After twenty-five years of biofeedback research, we can now demonstrate how negative thoughts and feelings undermine performance. Even slightly negative and pessimistic feelings make staying loose, calm, and positively energized impossible. Positive thinkers are better competitors.

Enjoyment

The principle is simple—when you can enjoy, you can perform. When playing your sport ceases to be fun, performance problems are inevitable. You can bet on it! It's the old chicken and the egg story again. If you believe you had fun because you played well, you've got it backwards. You played well precisely *because* you had fun. And there's a big difference.

Having fun and enjoying yourself is an essential key to staying relaxed, calm, unanxious, positively energized, and optimistic. It represents a boundless energy source for which there is no truly adequate substitute. As you will learn, having fun and enjoying yourself is a highly controllable feeling. Our best competitors go well beyond loving to win. They have learned to love the struggle, the battle, the confrontation. To love winning is easy; to love the struggle makes a great competition.

Effortless

As a young player I didn't understand that playing well can't be forced. When things didn't go well, and they frequently didn't, I had only one response—*try harder!* No one ever suggested that *trying softer* might be the answer. Trying harder often translates into tight muscles and a fast and frantic mental state. There is a big difference, I have since learned, between trying too hard and giving 100 percent effort. To perform well, I must give myself fully to the task, but I also must let go and "let it happen by itself." When things are going poorly, rather than trying harder, athletes consistently find that trying softer and easier enables them to continue upward and forward. As ironic as it may sound, playing well is effortless and will occur most readily when you give 100 percent effort to the task of letting it happen by itself. And trying softer and easier is learned.

> *John Brodie reported that when*
> *he was playing extremely well, time*
> *seemed to slow down.*
> *Everyone and everything started*
> *to appear in slow motion. The*
> *charging linemen, his receivers,*
> *and even the ball itself took on a*
> *slow-motion appearance. When*
> *this happened, he could see things*
> *much more clearly, had all the time*
> *to pick his receivers and release the*
> *ball, and it all seemed rather easy.*

Automatic

I call it "the paralysis by analysis syndrome," and I was a textbook case. Playing by instinct was out of the question. First of all, I wasn't sure I had any. I was constantly trying to think my way either into a brilliant performance or out of a performance problem. It seemed impossible to let go and play automatically. But then, no one suggested that I shut out all information I had stored in my head. Being logical and analytical seemed natural. "Head still, tuck your elbow in, too straight, wrist too loose, follow-through too short, watch your feet, don't forget to concentrate," and the list went on.

Learning to "turn on the automatic" and play essentially by instinct is fundamental to becoming a mentally tough competitor. Playing by instinct is always swifter and more precise. A specific set of Athletic Excellence Training procedures accelerate this process.

His best performances occurred when he wasn't thinking, when he played automatically and instinctively. According to O.J. Simpson, thinking was what got him caught from behind.

Alert

Bright eyed and intelligent is another way of saying it. When athletes are experiencing their own Ideal Performance State, they experience extraordinary awareness. They report that, although not distractive, they become acutely aware of their own bodies, the position of players around them, of who's likely to do what, of where they are, and what they're doing. The ability to anticipate well, to read what is about to happen, and to respond intelligently to the present appears directly related to this heightened state of awareness.

Mentally Focused

The importance of concentration comes as no surprise. We've all heard it before. The ability to focus one's attention to a specific target and resist being distracted from it is central to performing well in any sport. Two significant understandings emerged from the study of performing athletes regarding concentration.

The first is that attentional control stems largely from the right mixture of calmness and high positive energy. In other words, you are likely to concentrate well when you are experiencing an inner calmness combined with high levels of positive energy. Attentional control is impossible either when the mind is in a state of turmoil or when it is not properly energized.

The second is that concentration rarely increases with conscious acts of trying harder. Athletes who are performing well typically are *not trying* to concentrate. It seems to happen naturally when the inner conditions are right, and that's where mental skills come into play.

> *Eugene Herrigel in his book* Zen
> in the Art of Archery, *stresses
> the importance of a moment-to-
> moment focus. His years of intensive
> study taught him that one cannot
> force the future. For the arrow to
> fly true to its mark, it must take the
> archer by complete surprise.*

Self-Confident

Again, this element comes as no surprise. The importance of self-confidence has long been recognized as a key ingredient in success. It is essentially nothing more than the feeling that you can do it, that you can be successful. It's the feeling that keeps you calm and poised when everyone else is racing and scurrying about. And it's nothing more than a feeling that can be cultivated and controlled.

In Control

This last of the twelve ingredients is simply the feeling that "I am in control of me." When athletes are in the Ideal Performance State, they often experience a characteristic feeling of inner strength and self-control. It is the feeling of being in control of the situation rather than the situation being in control of you.

There are many things that occur during competition that you cannot control but you, in fact, can stay in complete control by controlling your emotional response to those events. Emotional control is the ultimate control.

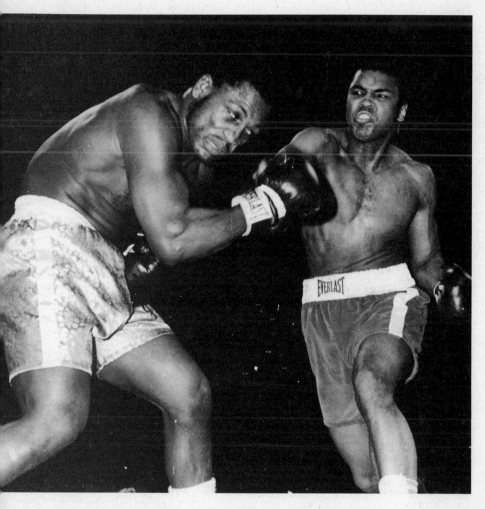

Few athletes have ever exuded more positivism, optimism, and self-confidence than Muhammad Ali. He clearly understood the importance of staying loose, energized, and automatic.

PRESSURE, PRESSURE, PRESSURE

One of the most significant and surprising findings that emerged from the reports of performing athletes was that mentally tough competitors *do not* play well under pressure. The finding was that nobody plays well under pressure—not even the superstars. Skillful competitors play well in pressure situations *precisely because* they have eliminated the pressure. The fans may be wild and the sportscasters close to swallowing their microphones, but the players who are doing well are in a completely different place psychologically.

Athletes reported that, although they were intellectually aware they were in a tough situation, they didn't feel the pressure on the inside. If they played well during a crisis, it meant they were able to continue feeling on the inside the same as they did before the crisis. What that means in terms of the AET model is that athletes perform best in pressure situations when they are able to successfully maintain their own Ideal Performance State. And that means they don't feel the pressure.

Why Don't They Feel the Pressure?

If you remember only one point from this entire book, the one that would help you most is this understanding:

> *Pressure is something you put*
> *on yourself.*

The only difference between playing a sport competitively and playing it for fun is pressure. For lots of athletes, playing for fun is easy and playing competitively is too much like work. For them, competition is hard, threatening, frustrating, and unnerving. But the game is played in exactly the same way in both cases. You keep score the same, the rules don't change, and you're often playing the same people. In most cases, the only difference is the difference you make of it in your head! Differences like, "One counts, and the other doesn't"; "My ego is really on the line in competition"; "What will people think if I lose when it counts"; the list goes on. These differences originate *in your head.*

You can structure situations in your thoughts so that it is impossible to play relaxed, calm, and positively energized. Competition can be

Pete Rose is an excellent example of mental toughness. His un-
wavering attitudes of hustle, 100 percent effort, and never saying
die have produced a remarkable level of consistency. His longev-
ity, he reports, is directly linked to his strong attitudes and beliefs.

just as much fun and just as pressure-free from the inside as social
play. When that starts to happen, you'll start becoming a mentally
tough competitor. As you'll see, it's your interpretation of what's out
there that gets you into trouble. There are no concrete, physical forces
working on you from the external world. Situations are not nervous
or anxious—people are. The sooner you accept that pressure comes
from within and not from without, the sooner you can start shutting
it down.

Disciplined Thinkers

Mentally tough competitors manage pressure well because they
have become disciplined thinkers. They recognize a connection be-

tween what they think and how much pressure they experience during play. Thinking the wrong thoughts, they have learned, can quickly lead to pressure problems. You'll never catch good competitors thinking thoughts like, "If I don't sink this putt, I'll lose $10,500." Or, "If I don't complete this pass, we'll never make the playoffs." Or, "The whole game rests on me—if I don't hit these two free throws, what will everyone say!"

It's always interesting to see the surprise on the faces of athletes when, through the help of EMG biofeedback, they can actually witness changes in the tightness of their own muscles when they do nothing more than change the content and structure of their thoughts. Skeptics quickly become believers. For some, it is the first time they make the connection between changes that occur in their heads and changes that occur in their bodies.

Sample Thoughts That Produce Pressure

- What if I don't do well!
- What if I blow it now; I'll never be the same.
- The pressure is awesome!
- I'll never live it down if I lose.
- If I don't do it now, I'll lose everything.
- My career is on the line!
- Just think of what I'll lose if I don't pull this one out.
- I'll drop all the way from second to tenth if I don't win this one.

Sample Thoughts That Reduce Pressure

- I'm just going to do the best I can and let the cards fall where they may.
- I'm simply going to focus on doing my job the best I know how.
- I'm going to have one hell of a lot of fun out there, no matter what.
- Pressure is something I put on myself.
- Even if I'm not the greatest today, it won't be the end of the world.
- Winning and losing is for the fans; I simply perform.

- I love tough situations; the tougher the situation, the better I perform.
- I'm going to be OK—no matter what.

Threat vs. Challenge

One athlete faces adversity and becomes bitter, frustrated, negative, and pessimistic. He finds all kinds of reasons why he can't perform—the coach, the management, his salary, the lousy team, and on and on. Everywhere he looks he finds reasons. Another player faces the same adversity and becomes stronger, mentally tougher, and more determined. His play becomes progressively more inspired and enthusiastic. In spite of the confusion and craziness around him, he continues to move forward and, in the process, becomes an inspiration to his teammates and to his coaches.

What's the difference? Why does one player fold under the pressure and the other seem to thrive on it? Again, the answer lies in how each athlete allows himself to construct the situation in his head. The difference is that one athlete mentally structured the difficult situation so that it became highly threatening, and the other successfully saw it as challenging. Whether situations are seen as threatening or challenging is under our own control, a control acquired by structuring our thoughts and ideas in positive, constructive directions.

Impact on the Ideal Performance State

When you perceive a situation as threatening, you will have Ideal Performance State problems. The more threatening the situation, the more serious the problems. Problems with muscle tightness, controlling anxiety, staying calm, and attention control are inevitable. Perceiving a situation or event as threatening triggers a predictable physiological alarm reaction, making your IPS an unrealizable fantasy.

The Physiology of Threat

Our bodies' natural alarm reaction triggered in response to a threatening situation may have been an important life-preserving response for our early ancestors, but for today's athlete it is a catastrophe. When our early ancestors perceived a situation as life-threatening, it generally was. Survival depended on an ability to make an immediate response. A lurking predator, a poisonous snake, or an approaching enemy produced a dramatic state of physiological and psychological mobilization.

The body had been put on alert to protect itself, either by fleeing from the threat or fighting. Pounding heart, rapid breathing, trembling body, elevated blood pressure, heightened fear or anger, braced and tight muscles, and tunnel vision are just a few of the consequences. This state of mobilization was automatic and involuntary, and was mediated by the activation of the sympathetic nervous system. Perceiving the situation as threatening was automatic, and so also was the fight or flight alarm reaction that was to follow.

Fortunately, there are no saber-toothed tigers in competitive sport. Unfortunately, our bodies are still responding as if there were. A third set tie breaker in tennis for $10,000 or an overtime free throw for the championship is not life-threatening. But the pounding heart, the rapid breathing, the trembling, the fear, and the tight muscles are all there. The athlete is fully mobilized for fight or flight but, in actuality, he can do neither.

A biological response that was at one time very adaptive and functional is now very dysfunctional. To serve an ace or sink the free throw, you do not need the adrenaline pumping. On the contrary, you need calmness, relaxation, positive energy, and self-control. To be successful, you must insulate yourself against that biological alarm reaction. Maintaining your own best internal performance climate once the alarm has been triggered is literally impossible. And the trigger is THREAT.

Controlling the trigger means controlling the way we think about the situations we face as competitors. We are not helpless victims of our biological instincts, nor are there actual physical forces in the world compelling us to react to stress in a particular way. We can control our internal reactions to changing external events. A major part of that process is constantly working to transform potentially threatening and difficult situations into exciting self-challenges.

"Why do I choke under pressure?" is a question I am often asked by frustrated athletes. The answer always involves one crucial understanding: that everyone, including the superstar, chokes under pressure. As long as you or anyone else feels the pressure, the alarm reaction will likely be triggered, and choking is the natural consequence.

Unlike many athletes, swimmers must break the pain threshold nearly every day. Maintaining an attitude of fun and enjoyment poses a great personal challenge. Breaking new barriers with yourself occurs when, in spite of all the obstacles, you chose to forge ahead and face the enemy—from within. Tracy Caulkins met the challenge and brought home the gold.

The key is to stop thinking about performing well or choking under pressure; focus instead on *eliminating* the pressure. It is this skill that separates the superstars from the troops—they have the ability to take the pressure off, transforming crisis into opportunity and threat into challenge. All that stands between you and that ability is your own head!

Raging Bull or Possum

When your biological alarm is triggered in response to a threatening situation, it quickly leads to a state of physiological imbalance. As pointed out, the physical and bodily changes which accompany the alarm response typically interfere with your efforts to perform to your peak. The cost, in terms of energy consumption, tight muscles, tunnel vision, poor judgment, and slowed reaction time, is too high. In contrast, the Ideal Performance State creates a special condition of emotional arousal that is substantially different from the kind of arousal generated in the alarm response. Both emotional arousal and physiological mobilization are required for peak performance but they have a different origin than the fight or flight response.

In an effort to find the right balance, athletes struggle between the extremes of raging bull and possum. The possum response, just as misguided and costly as the raging bull response, is very common. Athletes instinctively know they must shut down the alarm response to play well, and one way to do that, they learn, is to start playing dead inside. When they're dead inside nothing bothers them—they don't lose their tempers; they don't feel anxious anymore; they stay loose. From the outside, the player looks calm and cool. Until you understand the possum response, the fact that the player continues to perform miserably in competition poses quite a mystery.

Many of the Ideal Performance State conditions will be satisfactorily met when an athlete plays possum with himself, and that's what initially makes it so puzzling. A closer look, however, will always reveal that several important IPS conditions are not present, the most significant of which is the absence of energy and fire. In order to cope with his inability to control his emotions, the athlete simply puts out all the fire. Players are frequently accused by coaches, friends, and fans of being lazy, unmotivated, not playing with their hearts, and not caring, when they consciously or unconsciously use this strategy.

When this happens, the athlete often has a very forceful and angry response because, in his own eyes, he cares a great deal.

The fire must be relighted. Peak performance demands that the energy be there and that you remain very much alive inside. Maintaining the balance between "too much" and "not enough" is the dilemma. But, as hundreds of performing athletes have discovered, fueling the fire with joy, fun, enthusiasm, and team spirit builds the right climate inside (IPS) and, with it, the balance.

You Gotta Love It!

When an athlete can start loving adversity, then he or she is becoming a competitor! Adversity is the most difficult test of competitive toughness. Triggering our Ideal Performance State often seems so easy and natural when everything is going our way, when we're getting all the breaks, and when we're playing well. But adversity is always near, and our own internal response to adversity either makes or breaks us as competitors. The inner contest is won or lost in that moment. Through adversity we confront our strengths, weaknesses, and fears.

Adversity is:

- When you are on your opponent's home turf and a thousand fans have come to scream you into defeat—and nobody is there for you . . .
- When the weather is so rotten that you can hardly stand up—let alone play . . .
- When you've been sick all week and never got any practice . . .
- When your opponents get all the breaks and you get none . . .
- When everyone has written you off because you just don't have what it takes . . .
- When your personal life suddenly falls apart and you've got the biggest game of the year tomorrow night . . .
- When you're injured and you're not sure whether you can or can't.

These are the kinds of situations that often trigger feelings of anger, resentment, frustration, or nervousness. Situations such as these are capable of producing overwhelming feelings of pressure. Rarely do they produce feelings of challenge, inspiration, determination, and positiveness—EXCEPT IN TOP COMPETITORS! For the world's best, such a response to adversity seems almost habitual.

If you want to achieve your potential as a competitor, you've got to be challenged by all the craziness. In short—you gotta love it! And the crazier it gets, the more you love it. The greater the adversity, the more you feel the challenge, and the more you fight. Rather than dreading to play that certain person or team—you love it. Rather than panicking when the breaks go against you—you get inspired. Rather than playing timid or tentative when the door starts to close on you, you summon all the positive forces within you and eagerly charge forward.

That's what makes a great competitor, and that's what produces a real champion. Transforming adversity and pressure into challenge, inspiration, and opportunity begins and ends in your head. Set the wheels in motion and start loving it! Here's the first and most important step.

> *The next time you encounter the impossible craziness,*
> *clench your fists, get a determined smile on*
> *your face and, with all the feeling and emotion you*
> *can muster, say to yourself—*
> *I LOVE IT!*

The Importance of Rituals

Every good performer has rituals. Some are more obvious and elaborate than others. They're easy to see when athletes bat and pitch in baseball, serve and return serve in tennis, dive, golf, and shoot free throws in basketball. Although unrelated to the mechanics of a stroke or movement, rituals can become powerful triggers for creating the Ideal Performance State. They help in deepening concentration, turning on the automatic, raising intensity, staying loose, and more.

Unfortunately, when the game begins to go badly or when we start feeling pressure, we often short circuit our rituals. We start rushing. Even though we're not aware of it, we may bounce the ball less, take fewer deep breaths, visualize differently, and even cut down the time by half. In difficult or troublesome situations, we must be sure to take more than enough time to prepare prior to execution and complete our pre-performance ritual in its entirety.

Ask yourself the following:

- Do you have rituals that help you feel loose, confident, energized, etc.?
- Do you rehearse your pre-performance rituals so that they become powerful triggers for your own Ideal Performance State?
- Do you short circuit your rituals when things go against you?
- Do you study the rituals of top competitors in your sport that you admire? (They often serve as excellent models.)

THE RIGHT ENERGY

On February 22, 1980, the entire world witnessed the power of positive energy. Call it momentum, call it team spirit, call it what you will—it was *real*. When the United States hockey team defeated the Russians in the 1980 Olympics, you didn't have to be on the ice to see, feel, and sense the presence of something very powerful. Its effects were everywhere. For Herb Brooks and his "Boys of Winter," fear, anxiety, negativism, and self-doubt were nonexistent; there was only confidence, determination, self-belief, and joy.

What happened on that special day of the Lake Placid Games? It's well-accepted that the U.S. team did not win because of superior talent or skill. By most any calculation, they should have been outclassed by the Russians. But they weren't, and you could feel something build with each successive victory. On February 14, the U.S. upset Czechoslovakia seven to three. Two days later, Norway fell five to one. Could it really be happening? On February 18 Rumania was defeated seven to two, and then West Germany by a score of four to two. What couldn't happen was happening.

Minutes before the climactic Russian encounter, Coach Brooks summoned his team together for a few final words. "You're born to be hockey players; you're meant to be here. This moment is yours. You're meant to be here at this time . . ."

How did it happen? Some say it was destiny. Others say it was luck. But it was neither. The U.S. team simply outperformed the

Russians—they won because they played better. The U.S. team performed at the very peak of their physical skill and talent, and the Russians never came close to reaching theirs. What the U.S. team experienced and most of the world witnessed was the incredible power of positive energy. That energy became the ultimate force behind the victory.

The momentum, the team spirit, the positiveness, and the confidence combined to create a force that translated into determination and performance. The Russians were intimidated by it. Few could believe the level of performance attained by the U.S. team.

The Ideal Performance State became a reality, and it did so automatically in the presence of the right energy.

Positive versus Negative Energy

Regardless of your sport, in order to perform well you must be *energized.* The more we learn about what is required for top performance, the more we recognize the importance of differentiating between positive and negative energy. Let's look at the difference.

Athletes consistently report being highly energized during their best performances. They use words like "pumped," "psyched," "revved," and "jazzed" to describe the feeling. The high energy experience is also described as being very pleasant and enjoyable. An intensive study of hundreds of peak performances led to the following two-dimensional conceptualization regarding energy.

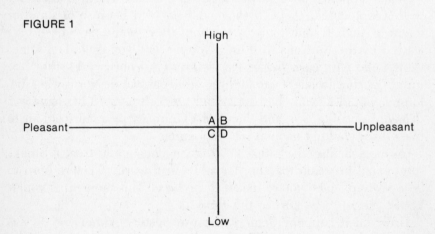

FIGURE 1

One dimension was from the feeling of high energy to low energy. Athletes' experience of energy runs from a continuum of super-high energy to no energy. The second dimension was from pleasant to unpleasant. Some states of high and low energy were very pleasant while others were very unpleasant. This second dimension, therefore, reflects the extent to which the particular energy state is or is not enjoyable.

FIGURE 2

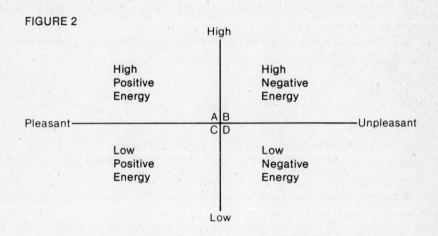

FIGURE 3

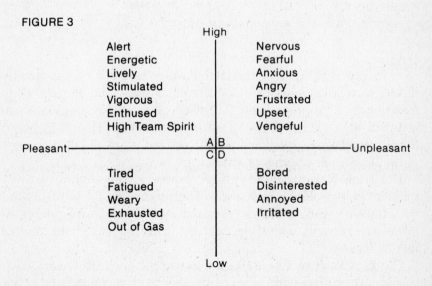

The two-dimensional model provided four cells that were labeled as follows: Cell A—High Positive Energy; Cell B—High Negative Energy; Cell C—Low Positive Energy; Cell D—Low Negative Energy.

Some states of both high and low energy are experienced in varying degrees as enjoyable—hence, the word positive was used; and some states of both high and low energy are experienced in varying degrees as unenjoyable—hence, the word negative was used.

Feelings expressed by performing athletes correspond to the four cells as follows:

Of particular note is that certain critical performance variables surfaced in combination with a particular energy cell.

FIGURE 4

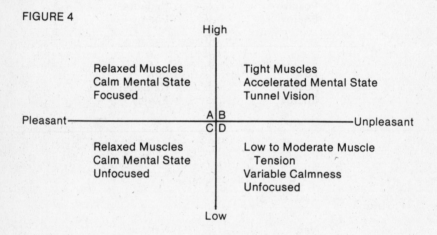

High

Relaxed Muscles
Calm Mental State
Focused

Tight Muscles
Accelerated Mental State
Tunnel Vision

Pleasant—————————————A|B—————————————Unpleasant
                         C|D

Relaxed Muscles
Calm Mental State
Unfocused

Low to Moderate Muscle
  Tension
Variable Calmness
Unfocused

Low

As indicated in Figure 4, the High Positive Energy Cell was directly linked to relaxed muscles, a calm mental state, and the ability to maintain an appropriate focus. The data collected indicates that some states of high energy do not lead to overarousal. The exaggerated fight or flight alarm reaction was not triggered in spite of the presence of the high-intensity energy state.

The High Negative Energy Cell, however, revealed an entirely different picture. Here, high levels of negative energy were associated with tight muscles, a fast, accelerated mental state, and tunnel vision—a very rigid, inflexible, and generally inappropriate kind of mental focus.

The Low Positive Energy Cell (low energy but still pleasant) was consistently paired with relaxed muscles, a calm mental state, but

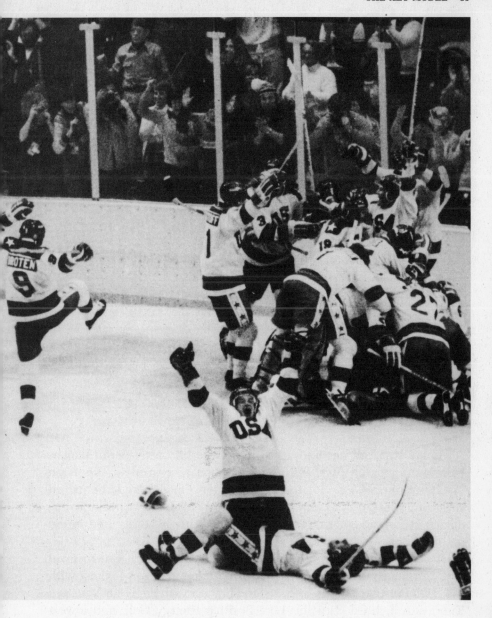

The U.S. defeated the Russians in the 1980 Olympics not because they were more talented but because they simply played better. The U.S. team performed at the very peak of their talent and skill, and the Russians never came close to reaching theirs. The team spirit, positivism, and positive energy became a force to be reckoned with.

poor concentration and focus. Here the problem was not tunnel vision, however, but rather one of being easily distracted. Athletes found their attention constantly wandering off to irrelevant things during play. They could be distracted by almost anything. Only with great effort could they keep themselves mentally on target.

The Low Negative Energy Cell (low energy that is unpleasant) provided the most inconsistency and unpredictability. Muscle tension varied from low to moderate, and mental calmness was highly variable. Considerable inconsistency was also reported in reference to concentration. Both tunnel vision problems and distractability problems were reported.

FIGURE 5

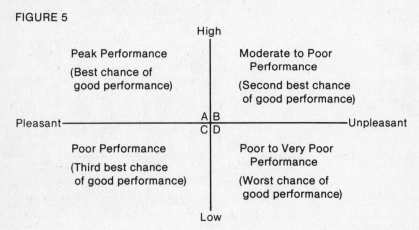

The most significant finding is that of the fifty peak performances first examined, all fifty, without exception, occurred in the High Positive Energy Cell. Not a single peak performance could be paired with any of the other cells. All subsequent analyses of peak performance experiences across seven different sports have resulted in the same finding.

Of particular interest also is the relationship of each cell to level of performance. The probability of performing well was highest with the High Positive Energy Cell, second highest with the High Negative Energy Cell, third with the Low Positive Energy Cell, and lowest with the Low Negative Energy Cell.

The data indicates that moderate to high levels of negative energy were preferable to low levels of either positive or negative energy. Performing well requires energy, and negative energy is better than no energy at all. Of particular note, however, in the judgment of either the athlete himself or his coach, the best performance reported in a High Negative Energy Cell was .60, slightly better than fifty percent of what was perceived to be that athlete's performance potential. In other words, on your best day you will only be slightly above average if you experience predominantly negative energy flow.

Performing to your limits, according to the data thus far accumulated, seems directly tied to the flow of positive energy. This is the energy associated with fun, enjoyment, determination, and self-motivation. When you love what you're doing, when you experience a sense of joy, optimism, or challenge in your play or practice, or when you experience high levels of team spirit, you're experiencing positive energy. The single emotion that best seems to describe the High Positive Energy Cell is that of JOY. In fact, in a significant number of cases, athletes used the word joy to describe the energy feeling during the performance.

In contrast, negative energy is the energy associated with anger, anxiety, hate, fear, tension, and resentment. It is produced in negativism and frustration, and spontaneously materializes when a situation is viewed as a threat. Figure 6 points out the relationship between threat and energy flow.

If you're highly motivated to do well, you'll generally end up in either Cell A or Cell B. If you're just getting started in competitive sport and you're highly motivated, Cell B (the High Negative Energy Cell) is where you'll likely find yourself a good percentage of the time. Even after several years of competitive play, some athletes consistently end up performing in Cell B. In actuality, you may move from one cell to another several times during a game or match.

The point is this. The more time you spend playing in Cell A, the better are your chances of playing well. And staying in Cell A is very tough work. Staying highly motivated and out of Cells C or D is sometimes tough enough by itself. Staying in Cell A and out of Cell B takes time and much effort. Managing the flow of positive energy is a learned skill that the world's top athletes have acquired.

In the workshops that I conduct with athletes, I have found it very helpful to assign a different color to each of the four cells. Colors were selected on the basis of their psychological impact and are used to facilitate the association of particular feeling states to the various cells. By repeatedly pairing a particular color with the feeling state to which it relates, the color eventually triggers the desired feeling state.

FIGURE 6

A deep, vibrant blue is paired with the High Positive Energy Cell. This color is often associated with calmness, strength, power, and control. A light tint of blue is paired with the Low Positive Energy Cell connoting calmness and pleasantness, but lacking depth and power.

The High Negative Energy Cell is paired with bright red, suggesting high intensity energy (anxiety, fear, anger, and frustration), but also suggesting the absence of control and direction. Black is the color of the Low Negative Energy Cell. It suggests no fun, no energy, no fire, and no life. This, of course, is the worst cell of the four.

Intensity Is Simply High Energy

Coaches and athletes are constantly talking about the importance of intensity in top performance. When asked, however, just exactly what intensity is, neither group can come up with a clear definition. Within the Athletic Excellence training model, intensity is nothing more than HIGH ENERGY. When an athlete is experiencing either high positive or high negative energy, he or she is intense. In the text of this model, then, high intensity and high energy, either positive or negative, are synonymous.

Obviously, our goal in top performance is to achieve the highest level of positive intensity of which we are capable. Negative intensity often results in a loss of calmness, tight muscles, and poor concentration. Determination, aggressiveness, effort, enjoyment, and fighting team spirit are the backbone of high positive intensity. Managing intensity levels is an acquired skill, and keeping the intensity on the pleasant side takes much practice.

For many athletes, the high positive energy associated with their best play is closely linked to strong feelings of aggression and determination. The intensity state is pleasant, but it is not a passive feeling of enjoyment. It is often a very active—"I'm going for it!"—feeling. The exact nature of the best energy state for each person is slightly different and must be determined individually. It is often, however, accompanied by rather strong feelings of aggressiveness and determination.

High-Octane Energy

An analogy is frequently made between the human body and a high-performance engine. If you're driving a Ferrari which requires extremely high-octane fuel and you consistently pump in the opposite, you shouldn't be too surprised when the result is poor performance. The same is true of human performance.

High-octane fuel is analogous to positive energy, and the human body is a sophisticated high-performance engine. Just as the Ferrari will run on low-octane fuels, so will the human body continue to perform with negative energy. The difference, however, is in the level of performance. For the Ferrari, low octane means constant maintenance, poor acceleration, unreliability, fouled plugs, poor mileage, and other performance problems. For the athlete, negative energy means poor judgment, tight muscles, early fatigue, poor concentration, and loss of control. The more you pump in negative energy, the more you will encounter performance problems.

Plain and simple: if you want peak performance, you must start pumping 100 percent high-octane positive energy. A three-quarter/one-quarter mixture of positive to negative energy may result in a good performance but not a great one. A one-half/one-half mixture will probably result in some performance problems, and anything less than a 50 percent mixture will likely be a catastrophe.

Maintaining a continuous flow of positive energy throughout an athletic event may at times be extremely difficult. Sports requiring aggressive physical contact, such as football or hockey, often trigger strong feelings of anger and resentment. Numerous situations during play, for nearly all sports, can trigger anxiety, tension, fear, frustration, or negativism. If, however, you have become skillful at maintaining the flow of positive energy, the effects of these negative factors will be minimal. A slight drop in your performance will likely be evidenced during these times but it's usually temporary. The problem is when these negative responses occur, and the flow of positive energy is already weak. That is when the performance problems begin to mount.

High-Octane Positive Activators	Low-Octane Negative Activators
Fun	Anger
Joy	Resentment
Love	Anxiety
Determination	Hate
Optimism	Fear
Enjoyment	Tension
Pride	Negativism
Self-challenge	Threat
Team Spirit	Frustration
Self-motivation	

When an athlete can't get psyched or energized from positive sources, he may instinctively resort to negative activators to avoid a completely flat performance. Have you ever played better when you suddenly got angry? Every athlete has experienced that at one time or another. Have you ever played worse when you suddenly got angry? That's an easy "yes" for most, too. The problem with negative energy is that a little is often too much. Getting angry or frustrated will certainly get energy flowing, but how do you get just a little angry, a little anxious, or a little negative?

Getting too energized from positive activators such as having fun, optimism, or determination is rarely a problem. You can't have too much fun or be too positive to play well.

With positive energy, the more pumped you get, the better you are likely to perform. The more you enjoy yourself and have fun, the more positive and optimistic you are, and the greater the team spirit, the better. Because you do not have to struggle as much with the balance between not enough or too much, your task is made significantly easier when you rely on positive energizers.

Remember, also, that athletes rarely, if ever, report playing to the peak of their physical skill and talent when they are energized principally from negative sources. The best they can attain is a slightly above-average performance. Peak performance seems to occur only when you are activated by such things as team spirit, enjoyment, and positiveness. What you are striving for is the highest level of positive intensity that you can muster.

> *Joe Greene described intensity as*
> *a state of wild frenzy but complete*
> *control. The intensity, he reported,*
> *was accompanied by a great awareness*
> *of everything and a feeling*
> *that everything would turn out OK.*

Averting the Flat Performance

How often have you heard coaches and players talking about "getting up" for the big game? "Getting up" simply means getting pumped with energy, getting properly activated. The consequence of not "getting up" for a game or match is commonly called a "flat performance." Players and coaches alike are constantly trying to devise strategies for averting this aggravating performance dilemma.

As you well know, "getting up" for the big game is not the real problem. "Getting up" for the "who cares" game is what is tough. When you're tired, not feeling well, or just burned out; when you're playing a team you've never lost to before; when you're completing a long road trip; or when you can't remember what it's like to win a game anymore, you're particularly vulnerable. These and dozens of other situations invite a flat performance.

Coaches instinctively try to inspire, challenge, encourage, and excite their players when they sense it coming. Some resort to threat, fear, anger, and intimidation to counter the obvious lack of energy—positive or negative. In the words of one famous baseball coach, "If all else fails, make 'em mad as hell."

It's interesting to note that when the effects of negative activation are examined for different sports, we find some rather significant differences. Sports requiring fine muscle coordination and balance (referred to as fine motor skill sports), such as tennis, golf, archery, and certain positions such as quarterback in football or goalie in hockey, can tolerate only relatively low levels of negative activation before performance is adversely affected.

For sports such as swimming, sprinting, bicycling, wrestling (referred to as gross motor skill sports), higher levels of negative activation can be tolerated before performance levels drop. With such sports as these, when an athlete cannot become sufficiently energized from positive sources, slight to moderate anxiety or anger may be helpful. Don't forget, however, there are some real risks involved with this strategy, and you will rarely perform to your full potential under these circumstances. Negative energy may be better than no energy at all, but it's still a poor substitute. The more you understand how vitally important getting properly energized is to your performing well, the sooner you'll be able to control it.

An Ancient Understanding

The concept of positive and negative energy is not new. It has existed for centuries. The Japanese call it KI, and the Chinese call it CHI. It is defined as the universal life force. Health, harmony, and fulfillment take form only through the proper direction and utilization of this life energy, which is said to exist in both a positive and a negative form.

To demonstrate the power and realness of positive Ki, Koichi Tohei, founder of the International Society of Ki, gathers his members together on the first three days of each new year. They travel to a nearby river where they all participate in a most unusual ceremony. As the sun begins to rise, all strip to their bathing suits, perform some light calisthenics, and proceed to follow the leader into the water.

What is amazing is that the outside temperature is typically around eight or nine degrees below zero centigrade, and the water temperature is barely above freezing. The members form a circle around the leader and calmly stoop until the water approaches their shoulders. They remain in the water for anywhere from three to seven minutes, and when the signal is given, all walk calmly to the shore. No one shakes; no one shivers; no one panics.

According to Tohei, this is not done to determine who can withstand the cold. It is a test to see how powerful the process of extending Ki really is. The experience also helps to wash away the negative thoughts and experiences of the preceding year, as well as helping to pave the way for the new year to be filled with positive Ki. When your Ki is a plus, according to Tohei, your thoughts, your actions, and everything around you will become plus as well.

Pumped Up but Calm and Quiet

I sometimes refer to this as the "soft energy." The distinguishing characteristic of positive energy is the accompanying calmness. You can be pumped with energy and still think clearly and remain calm. Negative energy has exactly the opposite effect. Being negatively pumped inevitably means a racy, fast, accelerated mental state. From the inside, it's like playing a 33 rpm record at 78 rpm's. Everything is too fast, and focusing on what's important is nearly impossible.

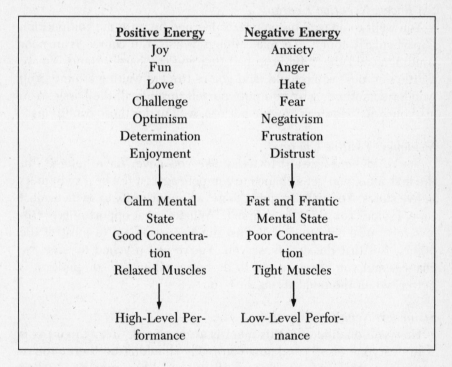

Positive Energy	Negative Energy
Joy	Anxiety
Fun	Anger
Love	Hate
Challenge	Fear
Optimism	Negativism
Determination	Frustration
Enjoyment	Distrust
↓	↓
Calm Mental State	Fast and Frantic Mental State
Good Concentration	Poor Concentration
Relaxed Muscles	Tight Muscles
↓	↓
High-Level Performance	Low-Level Performance

Everyone experiences the right energy a little differently. It also varies from sport to sport. The accompanying feeling, the intensity, and the character and dimension are often an individual experience. What is not individual is the calmness. Like the eye of the hurricane around which frenzied winds swirl, the right energy enables you to maintain a calmness and a stillness in action that is indispensable to top performance.

Examples

Ski Racer: Positive Energy

The wind bites across your face, and the snow is nearly blinding as you take your ready position. This is your moment, and you love every minute. You can feel that familiar tingling sensation up and down your neck. You are wired; supercharged. This is what you were born to do. You would rather be doing this than anything else in the world. This is your day, and no matter what—it's the greatest!

Ski Racer: Negative Energy

You want to do well but you're concerned because the competition is particularly tough. To make things worse, the course is in poor condition, and the wind is so bad that you can hardly stand. You're a little nervous, you're cold, and you're tired of waiting around. You wonder sometimes why you put yourself through all the hassle. You ask yourself, "How can anyone perform well under these conditions?"

Swimmer: Positive Energy

You're looking forward to today like you never have before. For the first time, you get a chance to compete against the best swimmers in five states. You're even going to get an opportunity to swim against John Taylor. You think to yourself, "What a great opportunity!" Objectively speaking, your skills just don't measure up to most of the others, but that doesn't phase you. You're just psyched to have the chance, and you always seem to do better when the competition is better, when the odds are against you.

Swimmer: Negative Energy

How you qualified for this meet is as much a mystery to you as it is to everyone else. You know you really shouldn't be there; you're outclassed. Many of your friends, family, and teammates are going to be there. If you just don't look bad or let anybody down you'll consider the whole thing successful. At least, today it will all be over with and you can start sleeping and eating normally again. Your parents say that you've been like a striking rattlesnake all week, but they understand you're under tremendous pressure.

Football Player: Positive Energy

You were humiliated the last time you played them. They made your team look really bad. This time will be different, however. You're better prepared, you've worked harder, and you know what you're capable of. You allowed yourself to become hopelessly intimidated when you played them three weeks ago. You're going to hold your own this time, and you are committed to keeping one central focus— doing your job the best you know how, no matter what. You're optimistic and excited about the confrontation.

Football Player: Negative Energy

You're still angry about the loss three weeks ago. The game tomorrow has become a personal vendetta. You really detest several of the players on that team, and you're committed to getting even. You get all tied up inside just thinking about it. You're convinced that they won that first game because they resorted to unfair practices and were just damned lucky. Tomorrow is your day for revenge.

Baseball Player: Positive Energy

You were pretty convinced that the new coach didn't particularly like you. He made it rather obvious both on and off the playing field. You really couldn't figure it out. Was it your pitching style, your personality, or what? Your anger and resentment started to grow. Even your teammates agreed you were getting a raw deal. You had good reason to get upset. But you suddenly seemed to get hold of your feelings and turn the situation all around. You became determined that this guy was not going to undermine your enthusiasm and desire for the game. You learned a long time ago how important being positive is to your playing well. You became convinced that your enthusiasm, spirit, and hard work would eventually be the deciding factor.

Baseball Player: Negative Energy

You've been in a slump for nearly three months now. Both your pitching and batting have been lousy. As you look back, it becomes obvious that your attitudes have played a major role. You were convinced that the new coach didn't like you, and that immediately put you on the defensive. Before long, you developed strong feelings of resentment. As much as the coach disliked you, you disliked him even more. Most of the other players agreed he was a real jerk. You often found it difficult to really give your best effort because deep inside you wanted to make the bum look bad. He took all the fun out of playing for you.

Basketball Player: Positive Energy

Winning the state championship was an unforgettable experience for you. No one gave you a chance of going all the way. Your team didn't have the height or the shooters to pull it off. But you could feel the momentum start to build from the very first game. The coach said your team had the greatest team spirit he had ever witnessed. Whatever it was, it made you and your teammates feel invincible— the team was supercharged. Negatives didn't exist. And there was a closeness that is hard to describe. Everyone was helping each other, building them up, making them feel good inside.

Basketball Player: Negative Energy

Your team was picked by almost everyone to win the state championship last year. Even you agreed no team had more talent. You had the big men, the shooters, and the experience. Why didn't it happen? You agree pretty much with your coach. It didn't happen because the players never came together as a team. There were just a lot of individuals out there trying to be stars. Everyone seemed to be jealous of everyone else. No one went out of their way to help anyone else. It seemed like someone was always criticizing something. Nothing was ever right. The bench was always quiet, even when you were winning a close one.

"Trying Not To" Rarely Works

Trying not to get angry, trying not to be nervous, trying not to be afraid rarely produces the results you want. Consciously trying not to allow negative energy to get started often results in low energy. You're simply substituting low intensity for negative energy. You may be successful in not getting angry or nervous, but the price you pay is equally costly—no fire. As we have already seen, you may perform better in a high negative energy state than in a low positive one.

Rather than focusing on trying not to get angry, nervous, or frustrated, focus on trying to increase your positive energy flow. In other words, going toward a goal produces much better results than trying to avoid one. When you face a frustrating or pressure-filled situation, start working immediately to increase your positive intensity rather than trying not to get angry or nervous. Playing not to make mistakes often produces mistakes and tentative play. Playing not to look bad or not to get your coach angry often translates into timid, low intensity play. Focus on playing smart, confidently and aggressively.

And the area of feelings is no different. Playing not to feel a particular way is deadly. Rather, decide what you want to feel—AND GO AFTER IT!

Momentum as Positive Energy Flow

Researchers have made several attempts to determine what momentum in sport is and how it is generated. Nearly all evidence collected thus far points to the conclusion that momentum can be traced directly to changes in the feeling states experienced by athletes during a performance. As you are well aware, momentum occurs in both a positive and negative form. Positive momentum in terms of the AET model is simply the intensification of those positive feeling states associated with the Ideal Performance State. When individuals on a team suddenly begin to feel increased confidence, optimism, energy, and alertness, they're experiencing positive momentum. And it can be triggered by any number of external events—a fumble by the opponent near the goal line, a great save by a goalie, or a breakaway and score by a forward.

Negative momentum is just as real. It starts when players begin losing those important feelings associated with their own IPS. They suddenly find themselves with low confidence, negative thoughts and feelings, negative energy flow, and a frantic mental state. The shift from positive to negative momentum can occur quite suddenly and unexpectedly. Just as positive momentum can make a poor team appear great, negative momentum can make a great team appear poor. The team or player who has it is rolling, and the one who doesn't is stalled or even falling backwards.

Mental Toughness and Momentum

Players or teams noted for their mental toughness and performance consistency have learned how to skillfully control the flow of momentum. When observing two championship teams or players in the heat of battle, you are likely to see frequent changes in momentum throughout the contest. And the shifting momentum will be predominantly occurring on the positive side, not negative. Good competitive teams and individuals are aware when their opponents suddenly start experiencing boosts in confidence, energy, and alertness. They, in turn, don't become negative, anxious, or frantic in response to it. They continue to maintain that special climate inside (IPS) and, with patience and poise, prepare for the opportunity to get the momentum back.

The key to controlling momentum is your own Ideal Performance State, and the most important dimension, as far as momentum is concerned, is maintaining the flow of positive energy.

> *The concept of positive energy, referred to as Ki, is central to the highly advanced martial art of Aikido. According to Koichi Tohei, founder of the International Society of Ki, "Many people set out with the idea of a positive approach, but a negative one comes boiling up and defeats them. In the training of Ki, we are always training ourselves to extend our Ki to make it easier to maintain a positive attitude. If someone falls into a negative state and someone tells us, 'Come on, remember to extend your Ki,' we get the idea immediately and can switch over to plus Ki."* [2]

THE RIGHT ATTITUDES

Analyzing the thinking habits of successful athletes for two years produced strong support for the following two statements: "Attitudes are the 'stuff' of which champions are made"; and "Mentally tough competitors are disciplined thinkers." The results showed that there is a constellation of attitudes which characterize the thinking style of mentally tough competitors. Attitudes are nothing more than habits of thought, and, as you must eventually come to understand, these habits of thought make or break you as a competitor.

As an athlete, you hear all the time from coaches, players, parents, and fans about the importance of attitudes. As boring as they might sound, they're right. But this will be different. You're going to hear more than "Straighten up and fly right!"; "Have you got a lousy attitude!"; or "Attitudes make the man and you ain't gotum!" For the first time in a long time, you're going to get charged up and excited about *mental attitudes*. Why? Because you're going to start getting *results*. You're going to recognize improvement in your performance almost immediately.

The Athletic Excellence Training procedures that you will be learning will be significantly more effective if you simultaneously work to acquire the right habits of thought. That's what this chapter is all about.

Thinking Right

So far, you've learned that if you can create and maintain a particular inner state, you have done the single most important thing you can do to insure your best performance. We called this special climate the Ideal Performance State. You also learned that your ability to control this special state was linked directly to the flow of positive energy. We're now going to learn how both the Ideal Performance State and the flow of positive energy are fundamentally tied to a particular constellation of mental attitudes.

As we shall see, the right attitudes serve to both stimulate the flow of positive energy (emerging attitudes) and help to control the flow

Merlin Olsen, respected as one of the most consistent football players in the history of the game, viewed every single play as an exciting new challenge in perfection. In his mind, he conceived each new play as the most important of the entire year. Merlin's performance consistency was a direct result of his disciplined habits of thinking.

of energy in positive directions (controlling attitudes). The right habits of thought, study shows, will unlock the keys to both positive energy and the control of the IPS.

Examples of controlling and energizing attitudes follow:

Controlling Attitudes	Energizing Attitudes
1. Pressure is something I put on myself.	1. I will always give my best effort.
2. Winning will take care of itself; I simply perform.	2. I take pride in what I represent.
3. Hard work can be fun.	3. I am going to thoroughly enjoy myself as I perform.
4. When I can enjoy, I can perform.	4. Having fun is an important key to playing well.
5. Choking is not a weakness of character.	5. My attitude is offensive rather than defensive.
6. I accept full responsibility for myself.	6. I strive to be positive and enthusiastic no matter what.
7. I simply focus on doing the very best I can at every moment.	7. I'm willing to pay the price, no matter what.
8. Mistakes simply represent feedback and are a necessary part of learning anything well.	8. I will be successful.

If I told you, as your coach, "John, here's what you have to do to play well. You must get out on that basketball floor and have lots of energy, low anxiety, be mentally calm, keep your muscles loose, stay mentally alert, be positive, enjoy yourself, have confidence, don't try too hard, and stay in control," you would probably proceed directly to the locker room and turn in your uniform. And I didn't even have a chance to tell you that was only two-thirds of the assignment.

What would your reaction be, however, if I told you that when you start thinking in a particular way, all those reactions will start occurring automatically when you play? Would your reaction be different? I think so. And the first step in having those automatic reactions is to reduce your negativism. As long as you've got the wrong attitudes, mental training exercises won't help your performance—you'll still get too tight, too anxious, too angry, etc., during play.

Reduce Your Negativism

My work with athletes has taught me this simple but absolute rule:

To achieve your fullest potential as a competitor,
you must reduce your negativism to a minimum.

Have you ever stopped to listen to how negative your inner voice is, and how often you're consumed in negative thinking? Often that inner voice and our habits of negative thinking become overwhelmingly powerful forces in blocking the realization of our potential. Unchecked, they undermine our confidence, our enthusiasm, our willingness to invest and persist, and, most importantly, our belief in ourselves. In short, our negativism erodes the basis of our INNER STRENGTH.

Remember, we function much like a very complex and sensitive biocomputer. We get back what we program in. Our patterns of thought and self-talk are important sources of input. You're either programming for success or programming for failure. Don't kid yourself into believing that your negativism is harmless. What goes on in the mind is reflected in the body.

The successful control of your Ideal Performance State and your ability to become a good competitor demand that you control your negativism. The following three-step process should help considerably.

- **STEP 1:** Listen to what you're saying and thinking. Become aware of your thinking and inner voice. Be particularly sensitive to any negativism. Start blowing the whistle on yourself as soon as any negative input is generated.
- **STEP 2:** As soon as you become aware of any negativism, shout STOP with your inner voice. You'll be amazed to find it actually stops.
- **STEP 3:** Replace the negative talk or thought with something positive and constructive.

Your negativism is controllable! Start taking charge!

The Attitudes of Success

- Attitudes Regarding Fun and Enjoyment

The Right Attitudes Toward Fun:

When I can enjoy, I can perform. To say that I had fun because I played well is putting it backwards. Having fun and enjoying myself makes playing well possible. The ability to enjoy myself in competition begins with the simple recognition that that is fundamentally important. If I work at it and make it a high priority during play, I can enjoy and have fun no matter how difficult the situation may be.

Impact on the Ideal Performance State:

Athletes consistently report that when they're able to maintain the proper attitude regarding fun during a performance, they stay relaxed, experience no anxiety, and remain calm, alert, and energized. Having fun is a powerful source of positive energy. When athletes are enjoying themselves, they typically feel "pumped up" with extra energy. And the more fun they have, the more energy they have available. Obviously, the fun that we're talking about is not the giggly or hoop-la fun. It is epitomized during play when an athlete can step back for a moment and say to himself, "I love what I'm doing—it's great!"

• Attitudes Regarding Winning and Losing

The Right Attitudes Toward Winning:

Winning is an important goal for me, but I understand that an obsession with winning is self-defeating. My efforts first and most importantly should be directed, not toward winning, but toward performing to the very best of my ability at the time. Doing the very best I can at any moment is my focus and my goal. Winning will take care of itself; I simply perform. In reality, I am performing against myself, not someone else. I will always be my own toughest opponent, and winning the battle with myself paves the way for winning the contest with my opponent. Winning the contest with myself and the external world becomes possible when I learn to establish the *right internal conditions.*

Impact on the Ideal Performance State:

This constellation of attitudes lowers tension and anxiety and helps produce the mental calmness so important to performance. These attitudes also help to improve an athlete's concentration and focusing efforts. This is accomplished principally by reducing tension and anxiety levels during play and providing a non-interfering target for the athlete to focus on as he performs, that target being "doing the best he can."

Note:

These attitudes concerning winning and losing generally eliminate most of the energy stemming from such negative activators as anxiety, tension, fear, etc. Most anxiety, tension, and fear associated with performance stem from concerns about losing, winning, looking bad, or playing poorly. The athlete, therefore, must seek other sources of energy, or he will probably perform very poorly (flat performances). This constellation of attitudes without other energy-producing attitudes will result in poor performance. In combination, however, with the attitude of having fun or self-challenge, the necessary conditions for top performance are quickly met.

The Wrong Attitudes Toward Winning:

Winning is everything. I have value only if I win. I am strong if I win and weak if I lose. Winning is good and losing is bad. I must win at all costs. I can't tolerate the thought of losing. I am a success if I win and a failure if I lose.

Impact on the Ideal Performance State:

These attitudes serve as powerful triggers of negative energy for most athletes. As we have already learned, this energy is extremely difficult to control. Over-arousal, together with all the negative performance consequences, is often the end result of these attitudes toward winning. With such attitudes, maintaining low levels of anxiety or fear, appropriate relaxation, and mental calmness represent nearly impossible tasks for most athletes.

Note:

Winning is the bottom line in professional sports. Winning is, in fact, everything! This realization, however, does not change the fact that as athletes become preoccupied or obsessed with winning, performance will show a steady deterioration in the majority of cases. Performance consequences are considerably better when you focus on performing to your best and then proceed to establish and carefully maintain the right internal conditions rather than focusing on winning.

• Attitudes Toward Mistakes

Winning is not normal, and those who win consistently follow an "abnormal" path. The discipline, the dedication, and the sacrifices are incomprehensible to those viewing from the outside. Joan Benoit wins because she deserves to win. She paid her dues.

The Right Attitudes Toward Mistakes:

Mistakes are a necessary part of learning anything well. If I don't make mistakes, I won't learn. Mistakes simply represent feedback. If I become upset, I cannot listen or adjust, and I am therefore bound to repeat. During play, I will keep mistakes and errors to a minimum when I successfully establish the right internal climate. There is no better cure for mistakes during a performance than the Ideal Performance State.

Impact on the Ideal Performance State:

These attitudes are tremendously helpful to the athlete in his efforts to stay relaxed and calm, to remain positive and optimistic, and to continue to experience enjoyment in his play.

The Wrong Attitudes Toward Mistakes:

Mistakes cannot be tolerated; if I'm tough, I will never make mistakes. If I punish myself for making mistakes, it will prevent me from making those same mistakes in the future. If I don't get upset with myself, I'll just keep right on making inexcusable mistakes. Dumb mistakes make me furious. Winners just don't make those mistakes. To be a winner, I must stop making mistakes. I must be perfectly competent and adequate.

Impact on the Ideal Performance State:

Since mistakes are an inevitable part of participation in sport, attitudes such as these quickly lead to anger, self-doubt, and a negative attitude. Over-arousal will be a frequent occurrence. The management of mistakes represents a major obstacle for a significant number of athletes, and it is precisely attitudes such as these that create that obstacle.

• Attitudes Toward Pressure

The Right Attitudes Toward Pressure:

I understand that pressure is something I put on myself. It is not something that just happens to me. Pressure and any resulting anxiety come from the way I choose to see the situation. Whether a situation is seen as a threat or as an exciting self-challenge is within my control. When seen as a threat, negative activators will come to the surface: tension, anxiety, fear. When the same situation is seen as an exciting self-challenge, a flood of positive energy is released, producing the opposite reactions. The ultimate challenge of handling pressure is the challenge of mentally reconstructing the event or situation so that it is seen as a positive self-challenge rather than as a threat. Transforming crisis into opportunity begins and ends in my head.

Impact on the Ideal Performance State:
The ability to see a situation as an exciting self-challenge rather than as a threat results in high positive energy while at the same time enabling the athlete to easily maintain low levels of anxiety and fear, mental calmness, and appropriate relaxation. Having fun and remaining optimistic is also enhanced.

The Wrong Attitudes Toward Pressure:
I have little or no control over how much pressure I feel. I've never held up under pressure very well. Certain people, places, and events are threatening to me. That's just the way I am. I really can't help it. I know I don't perform well in those situations, but it's not as if I choose to react that way. It just happens.

Impact on the Ideal Performance State:
With attitudes such as these, an athlete can quickly find himself victimized by pressure situations. Again, over-arousal will typically undermine the athlete's performance efforts. Threat and fun are simply not very compatible, but challenge and fun definitely are.

• Attitudes Toward Control

The Right Attitudes Regarding Control:
I understand that the finest athlete in the world in any sport will, on occasion, "choke." I can and will develop substantial control over it but I will never be immune. "Choking" is an indication that I'm out there trying, that I'm taking a risk. That's the only way I'll ever learn to control it. The more I fear "choking," the more likely it is that I will experience it. "Choking" occurs when I allow a situation to be perceived as a threat, triggering my biological "fight or flight" alarm system. It is actually nothing more than my failure to maintain the right internal conditions. It is not a weakness of character or flaw in my personality.

Impact on the Ideal Performance State:

Attitudes such as these produce poise and control. When the athlete finally recognizes that "choking" is nothing more than his failure to maintain one or more of the critical elements of the Ideal Performance State, he has taken a giant step in learning to control it.

The Wrong Attitudes Regarding Control:

Winners never "choke" when it counts. They don't fold under pressure. "Choking" is a sign of weakness. It is a true reflection of character. To "choke" is the worst possible thing that can happen. If I "choke," I'm not trying hard enough or not giving enough effort.

Another Version Can Take This Form:

Most things are caused by events and happenings outside myself. Luck or fate determines my future in sports more than anything else. My opponents seem to get all the breaks, all the good luck. When things go bad, I have little control over them.

Impact on the Ideal Performance State:

With attitudes such as these, the athlete often feels helpless as he struggles "not to choke" during competitive play. Anxiety and fear responses quickly become conditioned to pressure situations. The athlete begins to dislike competition, and when he does get involved in competitive play, he is quickly threatened, loses confidence, and generally plays poorly.

• Positive Attitudes

The Right Attitudes Toward Being Positive and Optimistic:

I have come to understand how important being positive and optimistic is to performing well. Maintaining a positive and enthusiastic attitude is a skill, not something that just naturally happens. I understand that with hard work, practice, and dedication I can gradually eliminate my negativism. Like so many important attitudes, it is a choice, and I've made the choice to be positive. I also recognize that eliminating negative mental habits takes time, but I will *make time* for this learning, and I will be successful.

Impact on the Ideal Performance State:

This constellation of attitudes, together with the attitude of having fun, combine to form nearly all the necessary internal conditions for top performance *by themselves.* Like fun, learning to maintain a positive and optimistic attitude has great value as a psychological training objective. Only after an athlete begins to fully understand the importance of being positive to performing well will he or she devote the energy and effort required to learn it.

The Wrong Attitudes (Negative and Pessimistic):

I can be positive if I'm playing reasonably well, but when I start making stupid mistakes, it's impossible. I'm a very spirited person. Some athletes are just naturally even-tempered and positive. I've always been a little negative but that's just me. I've tried being positive but it doesn't work. I've played really lousy, even though I had a positive attitude. It will take some time and convincing to get me to believe being positive is really all that necessary.

Impact on the Ideal Performance State:

Perhaps surprisingly, this constellation of attitudes is fairly common. The link between negative attitudes and poor performance is clear. With a negative or pessimistic attitude, being relaxed and mentally calm, with low anxiety and high energy, etc., is not possible.

• Attitudes of Excellence

The Right Attitudes Regarding Excellence:

I will always strive to give my best effort, regardless of the circumstances. I am never satisfied with giving less than 100 percent effort. I will always work to achieve the highest level of excellence I am capable of at the time. I have pride in what I represent and what I have accomplished as an athlete. Being true to myself and taking pride in what I do demands that I always give my best effort, no matter how badly the situation may have deteriorated. I'm not a quitter, and I'm willing to pay the price.

I've set goals for myself, and I'm willing to put forth whatever effort is necessary to accomplish them. If for any reason I should fail to accomplish my goals due to injury or some other reason, I will always know and take pride in the fact that I gave no less than my best. I fully understand that success is not waiting for something to happen, it's making it happen. I'm not content with simply holding my own. My attitude is offensive rather than defensive. I am active rather than reactive. I'm going for it!

Last but not least, I understand that my future as an athlete is in my own hands. What I accomplish and what I fail to accomplish is the result of me. I accept full responsibility for myself. My destiny is shaped and molded each day in accordance with what I dream, what I think, and what I do. I will be successful.

Impact on the Ideal Performance State:
This constellation of attitudes has two primary effects. It provides a very powerful source of positive energy, and it introduces a highly stabilizing control factor over performance. These are the attitudes that continually energize performance when things go badly. The energy generated from these attitudes is the only satisfactory substitute for the energy lost when an athlete ceases to have fun. These are the attitudes of a true professional, producing an element of control and consistency in performance that cannot be achieved in any other way.

The Wrong Attitudes:
I never get the breaks.
Nobody can work that hard.
It isn't really worth it.
So what if I gave up, we weren't going to win anyway.

Impact on Ideal Performance State:
Without the elements of pride, determination, and excellence, the high energy and control requirements will probably be noticeably deficient over a period of time. The impact of this on the Ideal Performance State should be clear by now.

So How Do You Acquire the Right Attitudes?

Attitudes are nothing more than habits of thought. Our attitudes are formed principally in response to the ways in which we consistently construe the world in which we live. Our parents as well as significant others in our lives, particularly in our young developing years, have a strong influence over the interpretation we give to our world of experience. If you tend to be a negative and pessimistic thinker, you learned it. Habitually thinking about your world in a negative way leads to the development of very strong and resistant negative attitudes. These negative attitudes can substantially alter the inner climate we are capable of creating as competitors.

Here are some examples:

- If you frequently *feel* threatened in competition, you more than likely *think* about competition in a threatening way.
- If you rarely *feel* fun or enjoyment in competition, you probably rarely *think* about competition being fun or enjoyable. Your habits of thought are blocking a particular way of feeling.
- If you consistently *feel* very undisciplined and lazy as an athlete, you probably rarely *think* about how disciplined and hard working you could and eventually will be.
- If you consistently become negative, frustrated, and angry in response to mistakes, you probably rarely think about how calm and cool you could be in response to mistakes.
- If you're frequently *feeling* negative and pessimistic about yourself and your future, you're probably not *thinking* challenging, inspirational, or positive thoughts.

As simplistic as it may sound, the key to changing attitudes is simply to start repetitiously thinking the attitudes you wish to acquire. Hundreds of opportunities arise each day to practice new attitudes. You may not believe them when you first start. The daily programming, however, quickly begins to impact your belief system, and eventually you will witness a very real and obvious change in the way you feel. The true test for determining *attitude change* is the corresponding *feeling change*. Here are some examples:

Repetitiously Say	Feeling Change
"I can do that!" rather than always saying, "I can't."	Begin to feel like you really can.
"I am getting more disciplined."	Begin to feel like you can become disciplined.
In the face of adversity say, "I love it!"	Begin to feel challenged, inspired, and strong as opposed to angry or threatened in tough situations.
"I love competition!"	Begin to feel more relaxed and calm in competition.

Here are some suggestions for acquiring the right attitudes.

1. Constantly repeat the attitudes you wish to acquire.
2. Read everything you can that pertains positively to the area you want to change.
3. Record the attitudes you wish to acquire on tape and play it back daily. Recording your attitude statements along with your favorite music is also very effective.
4. Make signs or posters with key words relating to the new attitudes such as, "I love it!" Place them in strategic places in your home or locker, e.g., bathroom mirror, refrigerator, etc.
5. As soon as you find yourself thinking the wrong attitude, say "stop" and replace it with the right one.

How to Think About Problems and Adversity

Competition is nothing but a continuous presentation of problems. Your emotional response to problems will bring you either success or failure as a competitor. If you expect to enter the competitive arena and have everything go smoothly, you're in for performance trouble. "Competition" and "problem" are closely linked, and to be successful, you must be a good problem solver. You must learn to control your emotional response to problems. Here are ways to begin thinking about problems so that you trigger the right energy response and sustain your Ideal Performance State.

- Problems will bring out my greatness—no problems, no greatness.
- I choose the way a problem affects me in competition.
- To become a good competitor, I must become a good problem solver.
- I never lose; I simply run out of time before I solve the problem.
- The right emotional response to a problem is 75 percent of the solution.
- Everyone is mentally tough when there are no problems; problems are a true test of my emotional skills.
- When I think I've exhausted all the options to solve a problem, I know I haven't.

- To love competition, I've got to love solving problems.
- I'm at my best emotionally when the problems are the worst.
- I'm getting good at turning problems into opportunities during competition.
- Give me problems—I need the practice!!

Don't Turn in Your Towel Yet

After having digested all the information contained in this chapter on the proper attitudes, you may be left with the feeling that this whole thing is just too much. Before you elect to turn in your towel, let me urge you to go a little further. This information will soon start making practical sense. The Athletic Excellence Training system, as you will see if you hang in there, is practical, understandable, and *works*. The material presented thus far is background information that sets the stage for the training strategies that follow.

> *"Far better it is to dare mighty things, to win glorious triumphs even though checkered by failure, than to take rank with those poor spirits who neither enjoy much nor suffer much, because they live in the gray twilight that knows not victory or defeat."*
>
> —TEDDY ROOSEVELT

THE RIGHT FOCUS

We get a lot of practice separating what we're doing from what we're thinking. Most of us have become experts at doing one thing physically and, at the same time, something different mentally. When was the last time you mentally stayed tuned in to your driving while driving your car? If you're like most of us, your thoughts drift a thousand miles away, only to come scrambling back to the present when a threat or crisis occurs. In a crisis, your thoughts come scrambling back to the here and now because instinctively you know that, to perform to your best, you must be mindful of what you're doing;

your thoughts and actions must be the same. You have the best chance of averting a fatal accident in such a crisis when you become totally mindful and aware of what you're doing at the present. Focusing on what *will happen* if you crash or fretting over why you decided to take this route will only serve to undermine your best response.

With just a little reflection, you can see that we have become masters at living somewhere other than the present in our own thoughts. When we eat, we ordinarily don't focus on our eating; when we walk, we don't focus on our walking; and so it goes throughout the day. For whatever reason, whether it's too boring or whether we're too busy, we're just not accustomed to keeping our thoughts and actions together. But isn't it true that we immediately return to that special focus when the situation suddenly demands our best response?

Consider, for instance, the mountain climber inching his way up a 2000-foot sheer canyon wall, the race car driver weaving in and out of traffic as he accelerates to speeds of 200 miles per hour, or the karate specialist who is about to break twelve one-inch concrete blocks with his bare hand—without question, their focus is moment-to-moment. Each one in his own way diligently struggles to hold on to the present and to appropriately focus as he acts. His very survival is often linked to it.

We often fail to recognize the importance of this concept to our own performance as athletes. We fail to be *MINDFUL* as we perform. Our thoughts are constantly drifting forward or backward in time to such things as past mistakes, winning or losing, what people will think, winning the next point, and what will happen "if."

As a receiver in football, we stay *with the moment* until the ball nearly reaches our hands, and suddenly our thoughts turn to running for a touchdown. As a result, we drop the ball. As a golfer attempting a delicate putt, we remain focused for a moment, and then suddenly our attention shifts to whether or not it will be good. The shift in attention occurred before the putt was completed and the ball passed considerably wide of its mark. The archer thinks *RELEASE*, rather than simply increasing his awareness that he is releasing the arrow. Consequently, the arrow is several inches off its intended target.

Performing well requires that our focus be moment-to-moment. The presence of NOW must not be disturbed by a thought of what might be or what has been. To put it another way, the successful competitor must learn to savor every moment of play as an end in itself. Top performance requires a mindfulness from beginning to

Wayne Gretzky attributes much of his success to his ability to set meaningful goals, to maintain a moment-to-moment focus during play, and to have fun as he performs.

end. This comes simply with merging your awareness with what you are doing at the time. Each link in the performance chain becomes an end in itself, with full attention given to the activity until it is complete.

Very simply, incomplete movements follow incomplete attention. Rushing occurs when we lose "the moment" and begin trying to force the future. When you successfully stay with the moment, there is no panic, there is always enough time, and the finish is as important as the beginning.

From Mindfulness to Flow

When we achieve the right focus, when we are properly mindful of what we're doing, awareness and action merge. The Ideal Performance State is fundamentally tied to the occurrence of this merger. The word "flow" is often used to describe the consequence.

In 1975, a highly insightful article, authored by Mihaly Csikszent-mihalyi, appeared in the *Journal of Humanistic Psychology* regarding the flow experience. Since that article, the word "flow" has repeatedly appeared in the vocabulary of performing athletes as they search for the right words to describe their finest hour. Subsequent research in this area over the past six years has verified many of Mihaly's insightful observations.

According to Mihaly, flow becomes possible when we act with total involvement, when action follows upon action with no need for deliberate, conscious intervention. It is an experience of unified flowing from one moment to the next wherein we feel totally in control of our actions. Because of its relevance to the Ideal Performance State as well as to the kind of mental focus we are attempting to achieve, here is a brief summary of the flow experience as he describes it.

- Flow is that special state where everything that we do is right and easy and automatic.
- Flow often accompanies activities that are perceived as being particularly enjoyable and fun.
- Flow results from a narrowing of attention wherein the past and future are clearly abandoned and the *now* is all that remains.
- Flow is a consequence of the special union of action and awareness.
- Flow most commonly occurs during the performance of well-practiced and familiar routines, when action and reaction are so well-practiced that they become purely spontaneous.
- Flow is rarely experienced when a situation demands a response that is clearly beyond the limits of a person's skill and talent.
- During flow, movement simply seems to occur by itself, as if something else were causing it to happen.
- Flow occurs when a person is aware of what he is doing at

the time, but is not aware of his awareness. As soon as he reflects upon his awareness, the flow is temporarily lost.

• Whenever we shift our focus to that of an observer, viewing from the outside, the flow is blocked. Examples of this would be such statements as, "I can't believe I'm doing this" or "Is this really me?" or "I'm really flowing." Ordinarily, the flow can be quickly re-established by properly centering one's attention.

The Right Focus and Its Effects

We have the right focus when *what we are doing is the same as what we are thinking*. It's as simple as that. When this focus is achieved and maintained, the following reactions occur naturally:

1. Mental Calmness—The racy, fast, accelerated feelings come from focusing on such things as winning and losing, how you look, what's going to happen if, and so on. Athletes consistently report an inner calmness when they "stay with the moment."
2. Low Anxiety—Again, anxiety results from the wrong focus. No matter who you are, if you persist in thinking certain thoughts, anxiety is inevitable. Being mindful as you act reduces the experience of anxiety to a minimum.
3. Automatic—The right focus enables you to turn on the automatic. This is such an important consideration. As mentioned earlier, performing well occurs spontaneously or it doesn't occur at all. You can't think or analyze your way to a top performance. The right focus, staying with the moment, insures that you will not become involved in highly deliberate and analytical thinking during play.
4. Alertness and Intensity—Focusing as you act produces a highly intense mental state, the same intensity which accompanies your best performances.

The goal is a one-pointed form of concentration so complete that a total loss of self-consciousness occurs in the act of focusing. This leads to what is called a state of *passive concentration*, a state of automatic mental focus. This is in contrast to *active concentration*, a state of actively "trying" to focus on your target. Top performance requires that we move from active to passive concentration, which is experienced as a totally effortless and spontaneous focus. This is the deepest level of concentration. The mind is relaxed and *one with the target.*

An important understanding is that concentration is a *learned skill.* Another important understanding is that your ability to concentrate is closely tied to your ability to control the flow of positive and negative energy. If you have trouble managing pressure, you no doubt have concentration problems as well. Figure 7 shows the relationship between energy flow and concentration.

FIGURE 7

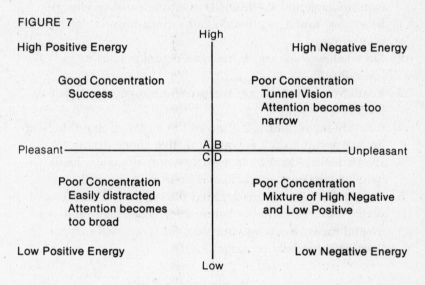

As indicated by the graph, you will concentrate poorly at both high and low levels of negative energy and low levels of positive energy. Your ability to concentrate will become increasingly more difficult as you get anxious or angry (high negative energy), bored or disinterested (low negative energy), or physically tired or fatigued (low positive energy).

With low levels of energy, your attention often becomes too broad. You're unable to limit your focus, and you become distracted by everything. With an excess of negative energy, your attention becomes too narrow. At times you may appear as if you're playing with blinders on. Your attention can become fixated on something inappropriate—a bad line call, the personality of your opponent, or your own nervousness or fear. As you relax and begin to lower negative energy levels, the situation quickly changes.

Concentration Strategies During Play

If you are concentrating and performing well, don't think about concentration—*just perform*. When problems develop, following these steps will prove helpful:

1. Check your energy level. Note the kind of energy you are experiencing and its intensity. Get the positive energy flowing as much as possible and reduce negative energy to a minimum.
2. Do whatever you can to become completely calm and quiet inside.
3. Focus your attention on the present moment, not past or future.
4. Actively focus your attention to the target. Being totally attentive and mindful as you act (active concentration) will spontaneously lead to an effortless and automatic focus (passive concentration). This is your ultimate goal.
5. Keep your eyes very controlled during play. There is a very close connection between your visual focus and your mental focus. Keeping your eyes on target will help to keep you mentally on target.

Concentration Strategies Off the Athletic Field

1. Improve your calming and quieting skills. This generally leads directly to improved concentration skills.
2. Practice meditation. Significant numbers of athletes have reported that in addition to improving relaxation skills, meditation serves as a form of concentration practice. For example, Billie Jean King reports using a tennis ball as her object of focus for fifteen to twenty minutes prior to playing.
3. Any activity that requires that you focus your full attention as you act can improve concentration. Concentration in sport is really the ability to remain totally *MINDFUL* dur-

ing action. Focusing fully on your walking as you walk or focusing fully on your eating as you eat are examples.

4. Practice focusing your awareness, being totally mindful, in difficult or tough situations. Numerous opportunities arise each day to rehearse this skill. Focusing your attention under fire is precisely what is required of you to perform well in competition.

Special Notes

Focus will improve with regular practice.

Every sport has a different set of focusing requirements. The mental focusing method described in this chapter applies whenever you are actually performing the activity. For instance, if you're a diver, you may mentally rehearse the dive in your mind just before you start your dive, or you may use any particular visualization technique that has proved helpful just prior to execution. As soon as you begin your dive, however, you should immediately establish the kind of mental focus described here. There are many times during play when planning strategy, shot selection, or error correction may be most appropriate. As soon as you actually begin performing, however, establish a moment-to-moment focus—there is no substitute.

CHAPTER III
THE PRIMARY
AET PROCEDURES

CONTROLLING YOUR IDEAL PERFORMANCE STATE

As indicated earlier, top performing athletes frequently are only vaguely aware of the existence of a special internal performance state. They often misunderstand what the state is and how it works. How, then, can they control something they aren't aware of and don't understand? The answer is that the control is largely unconscious.

What happens with mental skills is similar to what happens with physical skills. Have you ever asked a top athlete how he physically executes a particular movement or stroke for which he is noted? You might ask Borg how he hits his topspin forehand, or Wayne Gretzky how he shoots a slap shot, or Dr. J. how he hits a turn-around stuff. What you're likely to hear is not what they actually do. They may think they raise this shoulder and drop that one, rotate this hip forward and the other back, or tuck one wrist in and let the other drop—but they often don't know how they do it.

They certainly *can* do it, but they can't tell you exactly *how*. For the most part, the control they have acquired is unconscious and automatic. Hours and hours of practice and play have resulted in a highly complicated and efficient series of movements that can be executed without any conscious intervention. "It's almost as if I weren't doing it, as if someone else were doing it for me."

Exactly the same phenomenon occurs with mental skills. Mentally tough competitors have achieved a remarkable degree of control over their Ideal Performance State, but the control is almost always unconscious. They can trigger it in and out almost at will, and the better the competitor, the better the control.

Trial by Fire

If you persevere, you'll learn how to compete. That's how most mentally tough athletes got there. They didn't meditate, undergo hypnosis, practice relaxation exercises, or see a psychologist to get mentally tough. Their secret was simply to play, play, play—under pressure. They acquired the necessary mental skills through trial and error learning. As they performed in competition, they were unconsciously practicing muscle relaxation, mental calmness, positive energy, focusing, and so on. Control of their Ideal Performance State became a natural consequence of time and practice in competition. And the learning was essentially unconscious.

As with most learning, some people acquire the necessary mental skills faster than others. Some proceed more slowly, but not because they can't learn or because they lack the intelligence. Rather, the wrong combination of forces blocks the process. For some, an understanding coach, supportive parents, or the right friends make the process easy. For others, however, the absence of these and other factors makes the process seem like an impossible task.

The casualties of competitive sport start here. If only those athletes could have hung in there longer, they would have learned the skills— but they couldn't. The price was too great. And there are many people between those extremes—between finding it easy or hitting an impossible wall.

For the majority of people, trial by fire is a lengthy and costly route. Let's minimize our casualties with an alternative process.

Accelerating the Process

The Athletic Excellence Training procedures you are about to learn are designed to speed up a process, helping you become mentally tougher in a shorter and less painful time period. For that to happen, we must make what has been unconscious—conscious. We must make a process that has been automatic and beyond our conscious reach both deliberate and accessible. Trial and error is not enough. To hasten the learning process, we must leave nothing to chance.

Again, an analogy between learning mental skills and physical skills helps. If, as a squash player or golfer, you go to a teaching pro and ask for help with a particular stroke or shot, he's going to start by making conscious what has been largely unconscious. He's going to start increasing your awareness of things you're doing right and things you're doing wrong. This is how he accelerates the process of change beyond that of simple trial and error learning.

Increased awareness is the key to accelerated learning in the mental area as well. It is the first and most important step you can take, for awareness and self-control are inseparably linked. Most significant self-change first takes root in awareness. Awareness provides feedback, and it is precisely this feedback that gives you the information you need to accelerate to new levels of self-regulation and self-control.

AET Awareness Training Procedures

Although the specific elements of the Ideal Performance State are nearly the same for all athletes and for all sports, the way in which these elements are actually experienced by a particular athlete is highly personalized and individual. The following six steps will help you identify your own Ideal Performance State.

STEP 1: *Describe in writing and in as much detail as possible what your internal psychological world was like when you performed in your FINEST HOUR.*

Think back to a time in your sport when you were at your best. Select the experience that is freshest and most vivid in your memory. Sit back in a comfortable chair, close your eyes, and, as clearly as possible, reconstruct the entire experience in your imagination. Visualize all the circumstances in detail. "See" the field or court, the spectators, referees, fellow competitors. If the weather was warm, feel the sun against your face; if it was cold, feel its sharpness.

Once you have created the situation as vividly in your imagination as you can, begin to focus on what your internal experience was like at the time. What was happening internally, and how did you feel inside? You may also find it helpful to focus on your moment-to-

Mary Lou Retton epitomizes poise, confidence, and balance. Achieving greatness with yourself also requires balance—balance in your personal life, in what you eat, in rest and relaxation, in work versus play, and in emotional control. A life out of balance produces no greatness.

moment feeling state as you perform this exercise. Intensely focusing your imagination on a previous experience can frequently trigger the same feelings and reactions that occurred in the actual situation.

Be sure to take your time—don't rush. Allow yourself a minimum of five to ten minutes to re-create the experience. Once you recall many of the same feelings and reactions that you had in the initial situation, slowly open your eyes and begin writing.

If you don't have a finest hour that stands out, reconstruct an experience that was one of your better performances. If you play several sports and are having trouble thinking of a situation for one sport, use a good experience from another.

If you can't recall an exceptionally good day for you in sport at all, and this happens, focus your attention on an experience in which you were at your best (finest hour) outside of sport. The ingredients of the Ideal Performance State apply to the performance of any activity, whether within or outside the arena of athletics.

STEP 2: *Describe in writing and in as much detail as possible what your internal psychological world was like when you performed in your WORST HOUR.*

This one is usually easier to remember vividly. Athletes rarely report that they can't recreate a worst hour. Unfortunately, failures tend to stand out more boldly than successes in our minds.

Again, begin the exercise by sitting back, relaxing, and then vividly reconstructing the entire situation in your imagination. As uncomfortable as it might be, allow the entire experience to become real again. Give yourself ample time to get the feelings going. Once you have done that, slowly open your eyes and begin recording what your internal psychological world was like during the performance. Be as specific and detailed as you can.

STEP 3: *Fill out the following descriptive information concerning your FINEST and WORST HOURS by circling the number that best corresponds to how you felt inside at the time.*

You may wish to refer back to your written material if there is some question in your mind as to how you actually felt. Each category represents a continuum, such as feeling very relaxed to feeling very tight or feeling very calm to feeling very frantic. Circle the number that corresponds best to how you felt. For example, by circling number one on the first item, you would be indicating you felt very relaxed; a three, moderately relaxed; and a five would mean your muscles felt very tight. Circle only one number for each of the twelve categories. Try to give your best estimate of how you felt at the time.

For Your Finest Hour

1.	Muscles Relaxed	1	2	3	4	5	Muscles Tight
2.	Calm & Quiet	1	2	3	4	5	Fast & Frantic
3.	Low Anxiety	1	2	3	4	5	High Anxiety
4.	High Energy	1	2	3	4	5	Low Energy
5.	Positive	1	2	3	4	5	Negative
6.	Highly Enjoyable	1	2	3	4	5	Unenjoyable
7.	Effortless	1	2	3	4	5	Great Effort
8.	Automatic	1	2	3	4	5	Deliberate
9.	Confident	1	2	3	4	5	Not Confident
10.	Alert	1	2	3	4	5	Dull
11.	In Control	1	2	3	4	5	Out of Control
12.	Focused	1	2	3	4	5	Unfocused

For Your Worst Hour:

1.	Muscles Relaxed	1	2	3	4	5	Muscles Tight
2.	Calm & Quiet	1	2	3	4	5	Fast & Frantic
3.	Low Anxiety	1	2	3	4	5	High Anxiety
4.	High Energy	1	2	3	4	5	Low Energy
5.	Positive	1	2	3	4	5	Negative
6.	Highly Enjoyable	1	2	3	4	5	Unenjoyable
7.	Effortless	1	2	3	4	5	Great Effort
8.	Automatic	1	2	3	4	5	Deliberate
9.	Confident	1	2	3	4	5	Not Confident
10.	Alert	1	2	3	4	5	Dull
11.	In Control	1	2	3	4	5	Out of Control
12.	Focused	1	2	3	4	5	Unfocused

Once you have completed the first three steps, reread what you have written. Also compare how differently you responded to the twelve categories when considering your finest versus worst hour. Contrast the differences inside yourself when you're playing well to when you're playing poorly. Become acutely aware of how different and distinct the two feeling states are. As you start tuning in to your inner world of experience and feeling during play, you're going to start understanding how changes in your feeling states directly affect your level of play.

STEP 4: *Fill out an IPS monitoring card similar to the one following each time you play or practice your sport. Continue this procedure for the next three weeks.*

Type on either a card or piece of paper the following IPS monitoring categories:

IPS Monitoring Card

Name _____ Date _____ Time _____

1.	Muscles Relaxed	1	2	3	4	5	Muscles Tight
2.	Calm & Quiet	1	2	3	4	5	Fast & Frantic
3.	Low Anxiety	1	2	3	4	5	High Anxiety
4.	High Energy	1	2	3	4	5	Low Energy
5.	Positive	1	2	3	4	5	Negative
6.	Highly Enjoyable	1	2	3	4	5	Unenjoyable
7.	Effortless	1	2	3	4	5	Great Effort
8.	Automatic	1	2	3	4	5	Deliberate
9.	Confident	1	2	3	4	5	Not Confident
10.	Alert	1	2	3	4	5	Dull
11.	In Control	1	2	3	4	5	Out of Control
12.	Focused	1	2	3	4	5	Unfocused
13.	Played Well	1	2	3	4	5	Played Poorly
14.	Positive Energy	1	2	3	4	5	Negative Energy

Comments:

Make enough copies of the card to last you at least three weeks of play and practice, plus enough to cover your competitive performances for several weeks thereafter. Fill out the card as quickly as you can following play or practice. Obviously, your inner psychological world will change from time to time during play. The first half in basketball, the third period in hockey, or the second set in tennis may be quite different from other periods of play. In such cases, it is helpful to fill out more than one card. This enables you to more accurately chart changes in your feeling state with any simultaneous changes in performance.

If clear changes occurred, compare the differing periods of play. When you use only one card, consider it an average of the way you felt for the entire play or practice. Remember that you're giving your best estimate—a precise measure of your momentary feeling states is obviously not possible.

After monitoring your play and practice for a minimum of three weeks, continue monitoring your competitive performances for at least one additional month.

You'll benefit by giving serious thought in filling out your card. Although you could complete the card in just a few seconds, spend a few minutes considering each item. This particularly important step will accelerate the entire learning process.

STEP 5: *For the next three weeks, you are to substantially increase your awareness of your positive and negative energy flow during play and practice.*

FIGURE 8

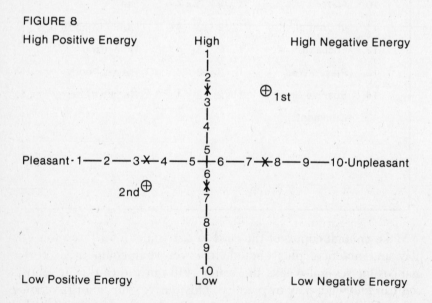

For each play or practice session, construct a graph depicting the four energy cells as shown in Figure 8. Rate yourself on a scale of one to ten on the dimensions of high to low energy and of pleasant to unpleasant energy. You may wish to mark each segment of the athletic encounter differently (e.g., the first half vs. the second half of a basketball game) if important changes occurred from one segment to the next. Once you've marked a point on both axes, extend the lines until they intersect, indicating the kind of energy and its intensity.

STEP 6: *For the next three weeks, you are to substantially increase your awareness of what your internal feeling state is like as you play and practice.*

You are, in effect, going to become an observer of yourself. The most important observation you can make is connecting how you feel *inside* with how you perform *outside*. Every time you play or practice, make a conscious and deliberate effort to understand how your level of play is linked to your changing internal feeling states. Here are some examples during play:

> *"I'm not playing very well right now. I wonder what's wrong. Let me take a look at how I'm feeling. I guess I'm feeling frustrated and a little angry. As I think about it, I'm feeling reasonably calm but definitely not having any fun. And I'm not feeling very energetic right now."*

> *"I'm really playing well right now. Let me take a look and see how I'm feeling on the inside. Let's see, I'm really enjoying myself, and I don't feel much pressure at all. As a matter of fact, I'm feeling very calm and relaxed. There's a real intensity though— I feel really focused and into it. I kind of feel like I'm on fire on the inside."*

> *"Right now, I don't feel much of anything. I'm really bored with this practice. I'm sick and tired of the same old routine. Talk about no energy, that's me. My play is real sloppy today—I just keep making dumb mistakes. Even though I know the coach is upset right now, it really doesn't seem to matter to me. I just want to get the whole thing over with today."*

> *"I'm nervous as a cat right now. I can feel my muscles are a little tight, particularly in my shoulders. Everything is going too fast inside. I can't think clearly—I'm definitely not very calm at the moment.*

*I've not made any really bad mistakes yet, but I'm
definitely not playing great either."*

*"I'm still so upset from that damn bad call by the
referee. I still feel like busting someone. I've got all
this negative energy pent up inside me and I can't
seem to let go of it. It's hard for me to focus on what
I'm supposed to be doing; I've already missed two
assignments. The coach is going to kill me. I can
really see how the anger is doing me in."*

From Awareness to a Three-Step Method for Emotional Control

Your ultimate objective is to develop control over your own Ideal
Performance State. Increased awareness will eventually enable you
to determine when this state is present and when it's not. You will
also be able to determine what elements are missing. Remember,
your Ideal Performance State is nothing more than a particular way
of feeling. At the most basic level, therefore, to become a mentally
tough competitor, you are seeking EMOTIONAL CONTROL.

The following procedures are valuable in accelerating control of the
Ideal Performance State. These procedures facilitate the learning of
a very special kind of emotional control.

STEP 1: *Relax, become very still inside, and practice triggering the
following positive emotions (feeling states):*

- Feeling of joy or fun.
- Feeling positive and optimistic.
- Feeling high self-confidence.
- Feeling highly determined.
- Feeling relaxed and loose (muscles).
- Simultaneously experience calmness, confidence, and high
  positive energy (joy or fun).

When conducting AET workshops, I introduce these training procedures by asking everyone to close their eyes and begin feeling joy
or fun inside. I give them only one and a half minutes to get the
feeling going. Usually, over two-thirds of the group are successful—
a surprise to almost everyone.

I then ask those who were successful how they were able to make that happen. By the ninth or tenth response, it becomes obvious that everyone did essentially the same thing. The emotion was triggered by focusing on a specific thought, image, sound, or sensation that at one time or another was associated with that feeling.

The trigger may have been a person's face, a particularly fun or joyous place, a bodily feeling, the sound of someone's voice, a particular piece of music, or some other pleasant experience. The emotion was elicited by controlling the thought or visualization. The more vivid the pictures and recall, the more intense was the emotion.

The objective in rehearsing feelings of calmness, looseness, confidence, and energy is to increase your ability to produce them during play. As with physical skills, the more you practice, the better you get. Ultimately, your objective is to be able to trigger a feeling state that contains all of these elements simultaneously.

In this first step, spend approximately two minutes on each feeling state. If you only have a few minutes to practice, select only a couple of the feelings and focus on them—perhaps joy for two minutes and then confidence for two. If time permits, proceed with all six. You will have the best success in the beginning if you close your eyes as you attempt to get the feelings going. Remember, you control feelings by controlling what you think and visualize.

Certain thoughts and images automatically lead to the feelings of joy, fun, confidence, etc. You must discover what those mental triggers are for you. Use sport-related thoughts and images to trigger the feelings if possible. If sport doesn't produce them, however, go outside the athletic arena.

STEP 2: *Practice the following visualization exercises.*

- Playing well visualization.
- Visualization plus IPS.
- Future visualization plus IPS.

Visualization is simply thinking in pictures rather than words. When you visualize, you use your imagination to reconstruct past experiences through images. You might call it controlled daydreaming. (See page 105 in Chapter 4 for more detail.)

For the best results, the three following visualization exercises should be practiced with your eyes closed, when you are in a very relaxed and quiet state, and when you are not likely to be distracted by noises or people. The time required to complete all three exercises is approximately ten to twelve minutes.

Playing Well Visualization

Recall, as vividly as possible, a time when you performed very well. If you can recall your finest hour in recent memory, use that. Your visualization is to cover three areas: visual recall, auditory recall, and kinesthetic recall.

Visual Recall—get a picture in your mind of how you look when you're playing well. You look different when you play well as opposed to when you play poorly. You walk differently and carry your body differently. When an athlete is confident on the inside, he shows it on the outside. So get a clear picture of what you look like when you are playing well. Reviewing film of past good performances helps to crystallize this visualization.

Auditory Recall— Listen in your mind to the sounds you hear when you are playing well, particularly the internal dialogue you have with yourself. There is often an internal silence that accompanies your best performances. Listen to it. What is your internal dialogue like? What are you saying to yourself, and how are you saying it? What is your internal response when faced with adversity during play? Recreate as vividly as possible all the sounds.

Kinesthetic Recall—Recreate as clearly as possible in your mind all the bodily sensations you have when playing well. How do your feet and hands feel? Do you have a feeling of quickness, looseness, speed, or intensity in your body? Often, your racquet, skates, bat, glove, etc., have a distinctive feel when you are playing well. How does the ball feel if you're a pitcher, the water feel if you're a swimmer, or the snow feel if you're a skier? Focus on any bodily sensations associated with playing well.

These visualization exercises are very helpful in building mental triggers for your Ideal Performance State. If you work at it, you will develop powerful visual, auditory, and kinesthetic triggers.

Visualization Plus IPS

In this exercise, you are to recreate a time when you were playing very well and simultaneously experience the internal feeling state that accompanied it. As you visualize, you should feel yourself becoming emotionally aroused—feel the confidence, the positiveness, and the intensity.

One of the measures used to determine how difficult a sport is from a mental perspective is the percentage of time the player is actually playing the ball. In tennis the figure is around 25 percent and for golf barely 1 percent. Golf is one of the most mentally demanding of all sports. Great golfers like Nancy Lopez have acquired superior concentration, visualization, and positive thinking skills.

Future Visualization Plus IPS

You are now to switch your visualization to the future. First, duplicate in your mind the conditions of play that you are likely to face in your next competition. If you know your opponent, the field or stadium, the probable weather conditions, or the crowd, add them to your visualization. Create the image of what you are likely to experience as vividly as possible. Now simultaneously trigger the emotional feeling state that accompanies your best performances, in other words, your own IPS. Fully experience that special combination of feelings as you picture yourself playing at your best. See yourself handling difficult situations during play, while remaining calm, relaxed, focused, and positively energized. Mentally and emotionally rehearse situations that have given you touble in the past. These may include getting off to a slow start, playing tentatively when you get a lead, reacting to personalities, or managing mistakes. Picture yourself successfully working through these tough situations several times. See it happen, and feel it happen.

Don't Worry—It Will Come!

Don't become discouraged or disheartened if you are having trouble triggering the desired images or feelings. Remember, you didn't learn your physical skills in a day. Practice and staying with the process will bring the results you're seeking. Practicing these procedures ten to fifteen minutes once or twice a day gets the best results, but even with a single practice session two or three times a week, you will see steady progress.

STEP 3: *From this day forward, every time you play or practice your sport, you must make a deliberate and conscious effort to create and sustain the internal climate that accompanies your best performances. In other words, you are to trigger your own IPS.*

This is the most critical step. No longer will you show up for practice or play and hope the mental skills will come. You are now taking direct control over the process, practicing mental toughness every time you play or practice your sport. And there's no difference between play and practice. Every time you enter the athletic arena you have an objective: to create and maintain your Ideal Performance State—NO MATTER WHAT! No more trial and error learning about your mental toughness. The objective, purpose, and path are clear. Make the commitment and start practicing!

The Power of Your Physical Presence

When athletes come to me for help in becoming better competitors, I strongly urge them to bring recent film of themselves performing. It is particularly helpful to review recent film of both poor play and outstanding performance. Important psychological understandings can often be generated by contrasting the physical presence of an athlete during good versus bad performances. How an athlete appears on the outside is often an accurate picture of how he or she is feeling on the inside. We walk differently and carry our head and shoulders differently when we are performing well compared to when we are performing poorly. Our look of intensity, determination, confidence, and calmness also takes on a completely different appearance.

I want athletes to know what they look like when they are performing well. I also want them to have a clear image of what they look like when the performance isn't going well and when adversity starts to bring them down. Athletes are often very surprised at the difference.

Outstanding competitors generally have a very powerful physical presence. They physically exude confidence, strength, calmness, and energy. The strong physical presence of a good performer often intimidates opponents.

Many competitors lack a strong and positive physical presence. Even when performing well, they may project feelings of low intensity, indifference, a lack of confidence, negativism, a poor self-image, uncertainty, or a general absence of inner strength. We can significantly improve competitive toughness by improving and strengthening physical presence.

When the physical presence of an athlete needs strengthening, ask the athlete if he likes what he sees. Do you like the image of yourself as a competitor? Do you physically project strength, confidence, and positive intensity? To help, I may show film of top performers they admire or respect. Does your physical presence compare positively to theirs? Invariably, the athlete picks up important differences. I'll ask questions like, "How are they communicating power and confidence?" "What do you need to add to improve your presence?" Eventually they come to see presence as a combination of the way they carry their head, their shoulders, the pace of their walk, and so on.

When working with groups of juniors, I'll often ask the group to give help to each competitor on what they need to improve their

competitive image. Peer input often proves to be helpful and insightful. It's very important in such situations to insure that the feedback
is always positive and constructive.

Once we have a clear picture of what needs to be added to improve
a competitor's image, we start practicing and rehearsing. I've worked
as long as two full days just to improve an athlete's walk. I want to
see confidence, determination, calmness, and fire. For most sports,
I want to see the image of a fighter. For the most part, I don't want
meekness or politeness communicated. Rather, I want strength and
confidence. We use mirrors, film, and video to help mold a powerful
image.

Why is physical image so important? The answer lies in understanding how powerful the link is between our minds and our bodies.
We cannot affect one without affecting the other. When changes occur
in our physical bodies, we will also have corresponding psychological
changes. To summarize:

- We can substantially control how we feel on the inside by
  controlling how we appear on the outside.
- If you want to feel strength, start looking on the outside.
- If you want to feel confident, start acting confident on the
  outside.
- If you want to generate positive intensity, start looking intense on the outside.

The principle is simple, but the results are powerful. Being a mentally tough competitor means controlling how you feel inside (IPS).
Three primary strategies accomplish that. The first is controlling what
you think; the second is controlling what you visualize; the third is
controlling how you look on the outside, in short, your physical presence. Make a commitment to improve your physical image every time
you play or practice your sport. Improve your walk, your appearance
of intensity, and your look of aggressiveness. Athletes rarely, if ever,
train in this area, yet my experience reveals its importance in building
mental toughness.

One reason why we outwardly display negative emotions is to let
everyone around us, including our opponent, know that we're really
much better than we're playing. We want them to know that we're
"off" and are capable of much more. "If I don't show I'm upset, they'll
think that's how I play all the time." That strategy may appear to

save your ego or pride, but it will eventually undermine you. Indeed, you rarely convince anyone, including your opponents, and you end up locking in the negative feelings. You continue to feel precisely like you act—miserable, upset, and negative. The performance consequences of those feelings are clear. Furthermore, when an athlete acts negatively, he often raises the confidence level of his opponents.

The message is clear. When the feelings aren't there, start acting "as if" they were.

Adversity is the true test of greatness. Mary Decker has been tested. Her total commitment and refusal to give up in the face of repeated setbacks give special meaning to her triumphs.

Act "As If" in Adversity

When you're feeling down, when the world has turned against you in competition, when you've lost your confidence, and you're feeling negative, fight the feelings by controlling how you look on the outside. Throw your shoulders back, pick-up your walk, and start manufacturing confidence physically. If you don't feel the confidence, start acting as if you do. That "as if" physical acting often triggers positive changes in the mental state. You can fool yourself into feeling strong, confident, and positive! And the converse is equally true. When you're feeling negative and out of synch, acting like you feel will lock in the wrong feelings. Remember, you can't always directly control how you feel, but you can always control your physical presence, and that often gets the job done by itself.

The final message: Work hard to develop and maintain the physical presence of a champion—no matter how you feel!

SUMMARY ROADMAP TO MENTAL TOUGHNESS

Mental toughness in an athlete is measured by performance consistency. Performance consistency is the result of emotional consistency. Those athletes who have learned how to consistently trigger a very specific emotional state during competition, referred to as the Ideal Performance State, are the best competitors. They have learned to respond to the continuous flow of problems and crises faced during competitive battle in a most unusual way. They respond in ways that keep them feeling relaxed, calm, energized, confident, and loving it.

How do they do it? First, they have learned to increase their flow of positive energy in crisis and adversity rather than decrease it. Second, they have learned to think in very specific ways. They have the right attitudes regarding problems, pressure, mistakes, and competition. Third, they have learned how to focus right. Their skills in concentration are exceptional.

How can we learn these same skills? How can we improve our own mental toughness? That's what the Athletic Excellence Training procedures teach. We can enhance our own mental toughness by adhering to these AET principles:

- Increase your awareness of the emotional state that is associated with your best performances.
- Practice triggering that ideal constellation of feelings both on and off the athletic field. The more you deliberately practice triggering your IPS, the more skillful you will become and the more emotional control you will be able to exercise during competition.
- Practice visualizing yourself in competition and simultaneously triggering your IPS.
- Take every opportunity you can in both practice and play to learn how to energize right, to think right, and to focus right so that your IPS becomes a regular reality.
- Remember, the benchmark of all great competitors is how they respond emotionally to problems and crisis: they become challenged, inspired, and more determined—they enjoy solving problems during competition.
- Improving your skills in visualizing, muscle relaxation, mental relaxation, and breath control will accelerate your progress in mental toughness.
- Keep a daily record of your efforts.

ATHLETIC EXCELLENCE TRAINING

Begins with Increased Self-Awareness

↓

Leads to

↓

Better Understanding of Ideal Performance State

↓

Leads to

↓

Better Control of Ideal Performance State

↓

Leads to

↓

More Emotional Control During Competition

↓

Leads to

↓

Increased Performance Consistency

↓

Leads to
↓
Increased MENTAL TOUGHNESS

Outline of Terms

AET: Athletic Excellence Training (a comprehensive mental training system for improving mental toughness).

IPS: Ideal Performance State (the ideal constellation of feelings and emotions for peak performance in competition).

MENTAL TOUGHNESS: The ability to consistently sustain one's IPS during the heat of competitive battle in spite of adversity.

POSITIVE ENERGY: The feeling of being energized and pumped up from your positive emotions.

NEGATIVE ENERGY: The feeling of being energized and pumped up from your negative emotions.

CHAPTER IV
REFINING YOUR SKILLS

VISUALIZATION TRAINING

Sit back, close your eyes, and vividly imagine the following scene. It's the bottom of the ninth, two away, men on second and third, and the score is five to four in favor of your opponent. To get into the playoffs, your team must win this game. If you don't, the season is over. You are next at bat. Although the tension and excitement are everywhere, you see yourself move confidently from the on-deck circle to the plate. The sun is warm against your face as you take your practice swings. The noise from the fans, the familiar feel of the bat, and the excitement of the moment are all very real.

In spite of the pressure, you feel confident, alert, and eager. This is a challenge for you, not a threat. You've been carefully studying the pitcher's delivery, and as you step into the batter's box to take the first pitch, you can see a slight nervousness in the pitcher's eyes. Now feel yourself in your ready position; see the pitcher's delivery; see the oncoming ball. You hear "Ball one!" from the umpire directly behind you.

You step back, take another practice swing, and then again assume your ready position. The pitch is right, and you swing. You can feel the bat as it collides with the oncoming ball. The impact is solid, and you know the ball is well hit—a line drive over second base. The runner on third advances, and the score is tied.

This is an example of visualization, a most fundamental and important exercise for every serious athlete.

Scenarios from athletes' lives readily support that. Robert Foster, for example, broke his own world record in rifle shooting even though he was unable to practice with his own competition rifle for over a year. How was that possible? He spent ten minutes every day for the entire year mentally practicing his shooting. Fran Tarkenton, one of the National Football League's greatest all-time passers, attributes much of his success to visualization. Before each game he visualized every possible situation that might arise during play. Jack Nicklaus asserts 50 percent of his performing well is the result of his visualization process. Bruce Jenner, winner of the 1976 Olympic decathlon, believes that his daily *mental rehearsal* of each event contributed substantially to his ultimate victory.

Most of the world's top athletes regularly practice visualization and acknowledge its value in performance. What they have learned, you can learn:

> *Visualization is one of the most*
> *powerful mental training strategies*
> *available to performing athletes.*

In many ways, we are much like image-sensitive computers. The mental images and pictures we have about ourselves and about what we can do and can't do determine how we respond and our corresponding level of achievement. Images serve as blueprints or roadmaps for our responses. If you program in negative and self-defeating images, that's precisely what you'll get back in performance.

Visualization is nothing more than the systematic practice of creating and strengthening strong, positive mental images. Call it positive image programming. It is a dramatically effective training technique for translating mental desires into physical performance.

A most insightful man by the name of Dr. Maxwell Maltz made an astute observation: your brain is incapable of distinguishing between something that actually did happen and something that was vividly

Jack Nicklaus attributes much of his competitive success to his
dedicated practice of visualization.

imagined. If you can imagine it vividly, actually "see" it, it's as if it
has already happened. When you vividly imagine playing well in
tomorrow's match, when you see yourself staying calm and relaxed,
controlling your temper, and so on, in terms of the information programmed into your central nervous system, it's already happened.
Thinking it paves the way to doing it!

Exactly What Is Visualization?

Visualization is the process of creating pictures or images in your mind. Whereas language is thinking in words, visualization is *thinking in pictures*.

Very simply, it is the use of imagination—"seeing" with the "mind's eye." It is the re-creation of past experience through mental images. In our use of the term, we include the re-creation of the feelings, sensations, and emotions that accompany those images. Visualization, then, represents the mental reconstruction of experience.

In visualization you need to *think in pictures*, not in words. Rather than *telling* yourself to get that important hit, to make the shot, or to serve an ace, you need to *see* yourself doing it. You create the picture and then copy the image.

What is particularly interesting is that you can simulate the conditions of competitive play more accurately in your mind than in physical practice. You can create fans, umpires, and opponents in your visualization practice, which is impossible in regular physical practice. You can *mentally* practice playing against the same person or persons you will face in your next encounter, rehearse the specifics of your strategy, and practice all your moves.

Athletes are aware of the importance of being mentally prepared in order to play well, but they are frequently unclear about what that means. Being mentally prepared for a game means NEVER BEING SURPRISED BY ANYTHING. An athlete who is surprised is frequently in trouble. You have the best chance of not being surprised when you have mentally rehearsed successful solutions to the many situations that may occur during play. In other words, you have developed strong, positive images for as many situations that may arise during play as you can. This means doing your visualizations.

Mental practice or mental rehearsal is often used synonymously with visualization. Actually, mental practice or rehearsal consists of picturing yourself *doing something* in your imagination—it is the rehearsal of a physical performance or movement in your mind.

The most important understandings in this area are as follows:

1. Everyone differs in his ability to visualize. Some can picture very vividly in great detail. Others can "see" and experience very little.

2. The ability to visualize is a *learned skill*. The more you practice, the better you get.
3. Visualization is one of the most powerful techniques to be used in learning self-control, self-confidence, and mental toughness in sports.
4. Visualization is the connecting link between mind and body in performance. It represents the most effective system of communication between mental desires and physical performance.

Under what conditions will your visualizations be most powerful?

- When you are in a quiet, non-distracting environment.
- When your mind is quiet and your body is relaxed.
- When you can set aside feelings, thoughts, and desires that are unrelated to the visualization.
- When you visualize in color.
- When you visualize in as much detail as possible.
- When you utilize your senses of smell, touch, feel, and hearing.
- Frequent repetition and practice.

There are two highly different approaches to visualization, both producing very different results. One method is to *become the performer* in your visualization; this is called *subjective* visualization. Here you physically execute the movements in your mind and mentally "feel" the results. In subjective visualization, the same muscles are activated in precisely the same sequence as would occur in an actual physical performance. This is an excellent method for rehearsing physical skills.

The other visualization method requires that you become an observer. With this method, called *objective* visualization, you view yourself as though you are seeing a movie of yourself.

Visualization Strategies

1. Practice visualizing and imagining with all your senses. Try to develop and sharpen your ability to create vivid mental pictures

of people, places, and events through practice. The more you practice, the better you get.

2. The more vivid and detailed your mental images, the more powerful are the effects of the visualization.

3. Use photographs, mirrors, film, or video replay to strengthen and improve the accuracy of the mental picture you have of yourself performing.

4. Mentally rehearse difficult physical routines, such as fielding, shooting, jumping, turning, or hitting, that have given you trouble. The physical practice of a skill, when accompanied by appropriate *mental practice,* is far superior to physical practice alone. Mental practice can help you to learn and master your physical skills.

5. Practice creating and strengthening *positive* mental images throughout all aspects of your play. Work to eliminate the failure images, and replace them with successful ones.

6. Mentally rehearse helpful mental and emotional responses to difficult situations that may arise during play. Rather than getting discouraged, angry, or anxious, see yourself staying confident, calm, and positive.

7. Work hard every day to change and reconstruct your negative and self-defeating self-images to positive and constructive ones.

8. Establish a regular visualization practice routine. For the best results, visualization should be practiced when you are very relaxed and quiet. Many short sessions (approximately five minutes each) are much better than one or two long sessions.

Visualization is not magic and does not take the place of hard, physical practice. There is no substitute for physical practice, but physical practice wins only half the battle. Thinking in positive pictures wins the other half.

SELF-MOTIVATION

A Systematic Approach

If you're having motivational problems, you're probably having performance problems as well. Motivation is the energy that makes everything work. Self-motivation is an important and powerful source of positive energy, and without it, performance withers. Progress, change, and top performance demand energy and effort. Your willingness to put up with frustration, sacrifice, pressure, fear, and hard work is directly linked to your motivational state. When you have permanently lost your desire and when you can no longer find a reason that makes sense, you are finished as a competitive athlete.

This is why you hear so much discussion about the importance of motivation and desire by coaches as well as players. It is the most critical factor in performance. Without an inner drive, working hard to change poor attitudes, to improve concentration or self-confidence, or to improve physical skills is useless.

Why do athletes lose their motivation? What causes players to burn out and lose interest? At the most basic level, this occurs because performing no longer fulfills or promises to fulfill their basic psychological needs, the needs for recognition, approval, self-worth, or success. In fact, quite the opposite may be occurring.

Playing competitively may stifle or threaten these basic needs to such an extent that the risk becomes much greater than the payoff. When the potential losses exceed potential gains, the player gradually begins to realize it no longer makes any sense. "Why work so hard, put up with all the hassles, stick my neck out, and then get nailed?"

Young or old, beginner or superstar, we are all potential victims of this trap. For the young developing talent, pressure is the force to be neutralized—pressure to win, pressure from parents, pressure from within. For the veteran, lack of progress or a perceived backsliding, with his or her declining years, hinders motivation. For the professional, not enough winning, not enough money, and too much physical punishment gnaw at motivation. To make things worse, lack of motivation is also highly contagious. If you are around people who have the motivation disease, don't be surprised if you start hurting yourself.

A Universal Antidote

What we do to maintain high levels of self-motivation, and what can we do to get it back when it's lost? The answer comes as no great surprise—SUCCESS. Success is a universal antidote. A word of caution, however: not success through the eyes of someone else. Success is the deciding force only when it is perceived by the athlete herself or himself. As long as you see yourself succeeding, moving ever closer toward the realization of another meaningful goal for you, you will stay motivated.

Your objective, then, is to program a diet of regular success. When the ratio of success experiences to failure experiences reaches a certain point, you're going to start getting interested again. The risk factor, the comfort index, and the profit potential have changed. Your involvement starts to have some genuine appeal again.

The Meaning of Success

Success comes at many levels. There are big successes, like winning Wimbledon or the Super Bowl, and there are little ones, like slapping the puck past the goalie on a break-away or sinking two pressure free throws to ice the game. All too frequently, the success of the little ones is muted by the failure of the big ones. Success and winning become scrambled. For many, when we lose, we fail, and when we win, we succeed. What a tragic miscalculation! The performance consequences are devastating.

In a world where winners are everything and losers are nothing, making the wrong connection is easy. The right connection pairs success with effort, accomplishment, and forward growth, not with winning the external contest. Steady success is the key to motivation. It's not a once-every-six-weeks affair; it's got to be constant. And big successes don't materialize overnight. They are the natural consequence of the accumulation of hundreds of little successes. As one of the premier all-pros in the National Football League wisely said: "You don't sneak up on success. You take it one inch at a time. We've all failed hundreds of times. Every man has paid his dues—some of us double."

Why, then, does anyone stay with it? What's the payoff? The answer, in a word, is *CHALLENGE*. It is having a dream of what you might do or become and then inching forward each day toward the realization of that dream. Each step becomes a significant success. The challenge of exploring and expanding your own limits starts the fire, and the fuel of success keeps it burning. If you take away the fuel, the fire slowly dies.

REFINING YOUR SKILLS • 113

Sticking Your Neck Out

There's another side to the business of setting goals that hasn't been discussed yet. Whenever you set goals for yourself, you also create problems, conflicts, and hard work. The act of setting a goal in itself is often a conflict because you're taking a risk with yourself, you're putting yourself on the line, and that's not comfortable.

When you set a goal of being a top competitor in your sport in five years, you are risking failure and you are creating mountains of hard work. You're also creating problems for yourself, problems of anxiety and tension, of controlling your anger and temper, of staying positive and optimistic, of managing mistakes, of handling failure, of time, of money, and more.

So, the next time you find youself in the heat of competition, and your elbow suddenly gets stiff, your hands start to tremble, and you even struggle to take a breath, step back and smile inside because you did it again. You put yourself on the line; you took a chance. And that's what it takes to be a winner—

> *Taking risks, making mistakes, and*
> *then finally breaking through.*

The Familiar Agony and Ecstasy

The joy, fulfillment, and satisfaction you receive when you accomplish another challenging goal is beyond description. It is the ecstasy of sport. But the agony is also present. You will, and probably already have, experienced considerable frustration, disappointment, and doubt. The key is to know and understand that it's coming and that it's a necessary part of the process. So don't run from it. Attack it. Fight it. Regroup, and shortly you'll break through, finding yourself ever closer to your goal.

A Guaranteed Program of Success

The program presented here shows you a step-by-step method for experiencing success every day, guaranteeing your self-motivation. If you will follow the plan presented here, you will experience steady successes, you'll stay self-motivated, and you'll find out how good you can be as a competitive athlete.

STEP 1: *Have a dream, a dream of what you could possibly achieve as an athlete.*

Every Olympic champion first had a dream of being number one in the world. What is your dream? Everything begins and takes shape from a dream. Your dream could be anything from being a club champion to becoming a world class player. It could be to change the long-standing negative picture you might have of yourself as an athlete into a positive one. The only condition here is that the dream must genuinely be your dream—not someone else's. Your dream actually is your long-term goal, something tangible and real, something to strive for.

Don't worry yet about being realistic with your long-term goal. What's realistic? Who's to say what's realistic for you and what isn't? Your dream is about your potential, and nobody can know what that is—yet. Not even you.

In shaping your dream, talk with top players, read their life stories, and learn from their dreams, hard work, and discipline. Have a hero, or several, someone who you would like to be like, someone to model. Your hero might be a superstar, a state champion, or even your teammate. Select someone that you particularly admire, and imitate his attitudes, dedication, and confidence.

Use your imagination. See yourself achieving your long-term goal. See it become a reality hundreds of times and the power of your imagination work. A very wise man once said that when a conflict exists between your imagination and your will, your imagination always wins. You can will a goal to happen, but unless you can see it, and dream it in your imagination, it won't become a reality. To achieve it, you must first conceive it, create it in your mind's eye. You must have a dream.

Don't underestimate the power of your imagination, both positive and negative. A positive imagination is the first link in the chain of success. A negative imagination is the most devastating opponent you will ever face. It represents programmed failure. Holding images of yourself as someone who never succeeds, who doesn't have what it takes, or who folds when the going gets tough is like one of today's sophisticated missiles locked on target. It's a predictable bullseye of failure. So hold on to your dream. Make it real. If it changes, change with it, but always make it positive and always see it in your imagination.

STEP 2: *Set intermediate goals.*

These represent stepping-stones to the realization of your long-term goal. Ask yourself, "What must I achieve during the next six months to several years in order to achieve my primary goal?" These all-important sub-goals should be challenging, exciting, and realistic.

Harvard psychologist David McLelland conducted an experiment that pertains directly to intermediate goal-setting. He devised a test called the Success Potential Test. The test consisted of six to ten people being asked to participate in a special game. The instructions were simply to toss a ring over a pin, similar to the ring-toss game children play. Each person got five tosses, and there were no other rules. The players could stand as close to or as far away from the pin as they wanted. McLelland found that the player who stood so close to the pin that he could easily ring it every time had little or no motivation for success. He also found that the player who stood so far away that he couldn't ring the pin more than once had little or no motivation for success. It was the player who stood somewhere between the two extremes, close enough that he could still have a good chance of ringing the pin but far enough away so that it was still challenging, who had the greatest potential for success. Consider these findings as you set your intermediate goals.

You should be achieving success with most of your goals in this category. If you're not, adjustments in your training efforts, time commitments, or goals may be needed. You may be setting unrealistically high goals. Guard against selling yourself short, but don't set yourself up for failure with impossible tasks. From time to time new intermediate goals may be added and some may be set aside. The important factor is to always move closer to the realization of an important goal.

STEP 3: *Set short-term goals.*

The champion and genius in you takes form here. This is the real battleground, where you finally become a winner or loser, a success or failure. This is your plan and commitment for today and tomorrow and for the next three to six months. These short-term goals are goals that, without question, you can achieve.

Here are some examples of daily short-term goals:

1. Complete your physical conditioning exercises each day to improve your stamina, strength, and flexibility. Specifically spell out what the exercises are, how many, total length of time of the workout, and so on.

2. Spend a specific amount of time each day working to improve weaknesses in physical skills.
3. Complete your mental conditioning exercises every day. Again, spell out when, how long, and specifically what the exercises are.
4. Always give 100 percent effort in practice and play.
5. Always maintain a positive and constructive attitude in play and practice.

Ask yourself, "Are these short-term goals reachable?" Absolutely! You can be a success with yourself every single day if you choose to be and work at it. Success is not far away; it is an everyday occurrence. Being a winner means breaking down your final goal into individual building blocks of success. It means designing a step-by-step sequence of success, one day at a time—great accomplishments *are* built on a series of small successes.

Training Assignment

1. Develop your personal *long-term* goal or goals. Put them down on paper. In your fondest dream, what would you like to accomplish as an athlete? The only necessity here is that this must genuinely be your goal—not someone else's. Being realistic is not important. This is simply your dream and belief in what you might someday be able to accomplish.

   My long-term goal(s) (goals that will take five or more years to accomplish):

   1.

   2.

2. Develop meaningful *intermediate* goals. Put them down on paper. These represent stepping-stones to the realization of your long-term goals. You should be achieving success with most of your goals in this category.

   My intermediate goals (goals that will take six months or several years to accomplish):

According to Bill Rodgers, running a marathon is essentially a
process of managing energy. When he is performing well, he
experiences the feelings of controlled strength, contained aggression, and positive momentum. He attributes much of his success
to his ability to set specific goals for various points during a race,
and his ability to maintain high levels of self-confidence.

    1. Approximate date when you will accomplish it _____.

    2. Approximate date when you will accomplish it _____.

    3. Approximate date when you will accomplish it _____.

    4. Approximate date when you will accomplish it _____.

    5. Approximate date when you will accomplish it _____.

3. Develop your personal *short-term* goals. Put them down on paper. These must be goals that you *can* and *will* achieve.

My short-term goals are (your plan of action for today, tomorrow, and the next six months):

    1. When_____ Where _____ How many _____

    2. When _____ Where _____ How many _____

    3. When _____ Where _____ How many _____

    4. When _____ Where _____ How many _____

4. Make a chart similar to the one below for beginners which includes all of your short-term goals. This is your way of keeping a record of your successes. Post your chart where you will see it, and check it daily.

My Short-Term Goals	S	M	T	W	T	F	S	S	M	T	W	T	F	S
			Week 1							Week 2				
Practice (2 ea. week)			✔		✔									
Conditioning (daily)		✔	✔		✔	✔	✔							
Lesson (1 each week)				✔										
Mental Homework	✔	✔	✔		✔	✔	✔							
Had Fun	✔	✔	✔	✔	✔	✔	✔							
Others		✔		✔		✔								

The above chart has been filled out for one week, and the person had twenty-four successes. This insures success, and that's the secret to *motivation*.

> *To become a champion, strive not to surpass your competition, but rather yourself.*

Those who consistently outperform themselves will ultimately outperform their competitors.

MUSCLE RELAXATION TRAINING

Every athlete who has performed under pressure understands how muscles can become tight and rigid. As pressures mount, the muscles enter into a partial state of contraction. When your muscles become overly tense, you will appear rigid, awkward, and less skillful. Top athletes are skilled in detecting subtle increases and decreases in muscle tension and then making the necessary adjustments.

A useful muscle awareness exercise involves monitoring the muscle-tension levels that accompany many common activities performed during the course of a day. These activities include driving a car, writing a letter, unlocking a door, cutting a steak with a knife, etc. How tightly are you holding on to the steering wheel? How tightly are you holding on to the pen while writing? How hard are you pressing? We often use far more muscle and strength than are needed to complete tasks efficiently and effectively. The goal in muscle awareness is *to match the task with the effort.*

This means adjusting muscle tension levels to whatever the task might be that you are doing. When we use too much strength, or when we "muscle" the movements, we experience a loss of quickness and accuracy. Early fatigue may also be an important consequence.

Mismatching the effort with the task happens frequently in athletics, especially in pressure situations. When you "muscle" a performance, the natural link system of your body becomes unmanageable. The arm locks with the shoulder, the hips lock with the legs, and movement becomes jerky and uncoordinated. As you inappropriately tense areas of your body associated with a movement or stroke, such as tensing your shoulders while hitting a backhand, the body's natural timing, rhythm, and flow become blocked.

Power, Muscle, and Relaxation

Hitting harder in sport does not always mean more muscle. Generally the opposite is true. Hitting harder usually requires relaxing major muscle groups, allowing the body's natural link system to function more smoothly. Power sport is directly linked to speed. *Speed is Power.* When an athlete tries to hit harder by using more strength, muscles become tighter, leading to restricted movement. How many times have you *consciously tried* to hit the ball out of the park in baseball or make your longest drive in golf by using more strength, only to find that both speed and accuracy were reduced. Your best performances will come when your muscles are relaxed and when the links of the body can flow freely and naturally.

Athletes' performances in running, weight lifting, and a wide variety of sports have significantly improved when they relaxed their jaws as they performed. Similar results have been obtained by requesting athletes "not to try quite so hard" or with four-fifths of effort, as opposed to five-fifths. This surprising improvement resulted primarily from the removal of excessive muscle tension associated with the performance. *Muscle relaxation is closely linked to maximum power and accuracy.*

"Muscling" is a poor compromise for loss of power and accuracy. The delicate timing and balance so often required in sport dictates another approach. The experience of "flow," so commonly accompanying a top performance, almost always occurs within a seemingly EFFORTLESS state.

In summary:

- Balance, coordination, accuracy, and quickness require muscles to be appropriately relaxed and loose.
- Quick reactions cannot be successfully initiated while muscles are tense and hard.
- Trying "too hard" frequently results in excessive muscle tension.
- "Muscling" a movement, in an effort to increase speed and power, will often produce the opposite results.
- Matching effort with the task generally produces an effortless performance.

Muscle Relaxation Training

Every successful athlete comes to realize and respect the balance between mind and muscle, between the mental and the physical.

Psychology has taught us that for every change that occurs mentally, there is a corresponding physical change.

Harvard physiologist Edmund Jacobson spent several years systematically exploring the relationship between mental anxiety and muscle tension. He later developed a training system that has become the cornerstone of relaxation training in sport psychology in the United States.

Jacobson found that, as a person becomes anxious and mentally uptight, his muscles will most likely show a corresponding increase in tension. Perhaps more importantly, he found that a person can learn to discriminate very small increases and decreases in muscle tension. He found that voluntary control of muscle tension is best acquired by increasing the person's awareness of when his muscles are tight and when they are relaxed. Not too surprisingly, Jacobson also found that as a person successfully lowered muscle-tension levels, his experience of mental anxiety would steadily decrease as well.

What does this mean to you as an athlete? It means two things. To control muscle tension you must:

1. Learn to control what you think.
2. Learn to discriminate increases and decreases in muscle tension.

To an athlete, excessive muscle tension can easily damage performance. In sports such as gymnastics, diving, golf, and tennis, where fine touch and feel are important, too much muscle tension can be devastating. The closer our muscles are to a resting state, the faster and more accurate our movement becomes. The lowest possible level of muscle tension that still permits the accurate retention of form and style is typically best. If you focus your attention on upsetting and disturbing thoughts, you will quickly find that your muscles are overly tight. You must learn to control what you are thinking, as well as to detect increasing or decreasing muscle tension levels. Jacobson's training program is included here to help you do that.

The Jacobson System—A Modified Approach

Jacobson's training procedures involve the alternation of tensing muscles and relaxing muscles, with the specific intention of developing an acute AWARENESS OF THE DIFFERENCE. The technique, you will find, is simple.

To "choke" at speeds of 200 mph could well be a life-and-death
matter. Race-car drivers like Rick Mears clearly understand the
importance of relaxation, calmness, concentration, and intensity.
Conquering fear is always a great challenge in high-risk sports
such as rock climbing, horse jumping, and rodeo bull riding.

The following procedures take approximately ten minutes. Follow
the steps below in the given order.

1. Select a comfortable chair, preferably a reclining one.
2. Find a quiet room.

3. Close both eyes, take two deep breaths, and feel yourself "let go."

4. Extend both arms straight out and clench your fists . . . gradually increase the tension level until all the muscles in your fingers and hands are fully tight . . . then relax . . . let your arms drop naturally. Be aware of the difference between feeling "tense" and "relaxed."

5. Extend both arms again, straight out, and tense the muscles of your lower arm and elbow . . . hold it, become aware of the feeling . . . now relax . . . let your arms drop naturally to your side.

6. Tense the muscles in your forehead by frowning . . . hold it, become aware of the feeling . . . now relax . . . let all the muscles in your forehead become smoother and smoother.

7. Tense the muscles in your face . . . grimace . . . hold it, become aware of the feeling . . . now relax.

8. Tense the muscles of your neck . . . hold it, become aware of the feeling . . . now relax.

9. Tense the muscles of the shoulders . . . hold it, become aware of the feeling . . . now relax.

10. Tense the muscles of the back, first the upper back and then the lower . . . hold it, become aware of the feeling . . . now relax.

11. Tense the muscles of your chest . . . hold it, become aware of the feeling . . . now relax.

12. Tense the muscles of your stomach . . . hold it, become aware of the feeling . . . now relax.

13. Tense the muscles of your abdomen . . . hold it, become aware of the feeling . . . now relax.

14. Tense the muscles of your upper leg—all the muscles of the thigh . . . hold it, become aware of the feeling . . . now relax.

15. Tense the muscles of your lower leg—all the muscles of the knee and calf . . . hold it, become aware of the feeling . . . now relax.

16. Tense the muscles of your feet and toes . . . hold it, become aware of the feeling . . . now relax.

17. Now concentrate on relaxing all the muscles of your body. Become aware of any areas that might still be tense in

any way, and relax them. Maintain this state of total muscle relaxation for at least two to three minutes.

18. Open your eyes, stretch, and feel refreshed . . . go about your business.

This systematic process of muscle relaxation, although quite simple, has proved to be a powerful and useful technique in helping athletes develop an acute awareness of muscle tension states and learn to control the effects of tension on the muscles themselves. This routine MUST be practiced regularly for mastery of the skills.

Training Strategies

1. Experiment with different muscle tension levels as you practice your sport. Try to discover the best zone of tension for your best performance. Practice executing critical movements in your sport with the different levels of tightness and looseness in your hands, arms, legs, etc. Determine for yourself how relaxed you must be to achieve maximum power, quickness, and accuracy with the least effort.

2. Determine the performance consequences of not enough muscle tension as well as excessive muscle tension as you practice your sport.

3. Monitor the amount of muscle tension that exists in your muscles when you are performing such common activities as driving, writing, eating or walking. Practice matching the effort to the task. Your objective is to use just enough tension to get the job done perfectly.

4. Practice Jacobson's exercises ten to fifteen minutes each day for seven days.

5. During the second week of practice with the Jacobson method, try to get your muscles to relax quickly without bringing muscle groups to a full state of contraction. If you are not successful, return to the original exercises. Repeat until you can relax all your muscles very quickly just by thinking certain thoughts.

6. Constantly practice raising your positive intensity to the highest possible level while simultaneously keeping your muscles relaxed and free.

Remember—your competitive goal is relaxation of *muscles*, not of your *mind*! High-level performance requires that your muscles be relaxed but your mind remain crystal clear and alert.

MANAGING NEGATIVE ENERGY

The Art of Managing Negative Energy

The finest competitive athlete in the world will occasionally find himself relying on negative activators for maintaining sufficient energy levels during play. He stuggles like the rest of us to keep from getting too frustrated, too anxious, too angry, or too excited during play. The main difference, however, is his superior skill in managing and controlling that energy. Top competitors have highly developed RELAXATION SKILLS. This is the skill you draw upon when you become too activated to play well. As you learned in an earlier chapter, when this happens, your best zone of arousal has been exceeded. The primary function of your relaxation skills is to lower your energy and arousal levels so that they do not interfere with your play.

No matter how mentally tough you become, you will inevitably perceive some competitive situations as partially threatening. Nor will you totally eliminate negative activators. Strengthening your relaxation skills is necessary to becoming a successful competitor.

Let's begin by examining some typical signs of over-arousal.

- Muscles become too tight and rigid.
- Fast heart rate, shallow and irregular breathing, often accompanied by a racy, accelerated feeling.
- Legs feel weak and rubbery.
- Difficulty in concentrating and focusing.
- Everything appears to be going faster than it really is.
- Inability to think clearly and accurately.
- Attention gets fixed on one thing and refocusing is difficult.
- Feeling of high anxiety and/or fear.
- Become fatigued very quickly.
- Become increasingly negative and self-critical.
- Decreasing emotional control.

Your ability to relax is directly related to your personal moods, how deeply you feel things, and how long feelings or moods last. It is also related to your ability to change from one emotion to another as well as to your ability to control emotional responses. Whatever these various considerations are for you, remember that they are all modifiable through learning.

The next step is to learn strategies for improving your relaxation efforts, both on and off the athletic field. Strategies for lowering your arousal levels *during play* include the following:

1. Deliberately slow your breathing as much as possible. Maintain a slow, regular pattern of breathing whenever the situation permits.
2. Take more time doing everything, and deliberately slow down.
3. Focus on doing the best you can—not on winning or losing. Try to play "within yourself," not against an opponent.
4. Stay within the here-and-now context in your thoughts. Focusing on either the past or future makes things worse.
5. If muscles become overly tight, first contract and then relax those muscles. Dangling your arms and hands to your sides and vigorously shaking frequently helps to "shake out" excess tension.
6. Focus your attention away from disturbing thoughts whenever possible. Focus your attention on the appropriate target. This will quickly help you to relax.
7. Play down the importance of the performance in your mind.
8. Keep a positive and constructive attitude. You are already over-aroused. Should you become increasingly negative or angry, the situation will quickly become impossible.
9. Create the strongest mental image that you can of yourself playing "in your finest hour." Recapture "the feeling" as well as you can.
10. Try to have fun and enjoy yourself. If you can momentarily step back and gain this perspective in your mind, negative activators quickly diminish.

"To become a champion requires a condition of readiness that causes the individual to approach with pleasure even the most tedious practice session." Bruce Lee felt strongly that mental poise and emotional control were closely linked to relaxation. Relaxation, he warned, however, was relaxation of the muscles—not of the mind or attention.

Improving Your Skills Off the Playing Field

Don't ever forget that relaxation is a learned skill. Successfully lowering heart rate, blood pressure, breathing, muscle tension, and brain wave activity are all part of that skill. You are practicing your relaxation skills every time you *perform under pressure*. That is, in fact, one of the best training strategies for increasing those essential relaxation skills. As with activation skills, if you practice off the playing field, you'll accelerate the learning process.

Autogenic Training for Relaxation

The following exercises teach relaxation by having you focus on the "feeling states" typically associated with body and mind relaxation. For all of the autogenic exercises, your eyes should be closed, you should be seated in a comfortable chair or lying on your back, and you should adopt an attitude of "letting it happen" as opposed to "forcing it." Spend about ten minutes on the exercise designated for that day. You may repeat the exercise two or three times during that day.

DAY 1: You are to arouse very vivid and enjoyable feelings of heaviness throughout your body in this exercise. Silently begin repeating, "My right hand and arm are becoming heavy." As you say it, focus your attention on the sensation of heaviness in your right hand and arm. Say it two or three times and finish with, "My arm and hand are completely heavy." Then move to your left hand and arm. If you have trouble getting the feeling, pick up something heavy and focus on it. Return again to the exercise. After you have focused on heaviness in your arms and hands, proceed to your shoulders, neck, head, chest, legs, and feet. Remember: *don't try too hard.*

DAY 2: You are to arouse a very vivid and enjoyable feeling of warmth throughout your body in this exercise. Silently begin repeating, "My right arm and hand are becoming warmer and warmer." Focus your total attention on the sensation of warmth. If you have trouble, get a mental picture of your hand submerged in warm water or warming in the hot sun. Say that phrase two or three times, and then move on to your left hand and arm. Proceed eventually to your entire body, including your feet and toes.

DAY 3: You are to produce a very calm, regular, and steady heartbeat in this exercise. Silently begin repeating, "My heartbeat is very calm and regular. My heartbeat is very calm and regular. I feel calm and steady." Continue repeating these self-suggestions for the entire seven- to ten-minute period. (Sometimes focusing on your heartbeat will cause it to speed up. Don't worry. Just relax, and continue your efforts; eventually you will be successful.)

DAY 4: You are to produce very slow, deep, and regular breathing with this exercise. Silently begin repeating, "My breathing is becoming calm and regular. My breathing is very easy and slow." Continue repeating these self-suggestions for the entire seven- to ten-minute period.

DAY 5: You are to arouse a very enjoyable and relaxed feeling in your *stomach* and *lower abdomen*. Silently begin repeating, "My stomach is feeling warm, calm, and relaxed. My stomach is feeling warm, calm, and relaxed." Continue repeating these self-suggestions for the entire seven- to ten-minute period.

DAY 6: You are to produce the feeling of coolness on your forehead with this exercise. (You may wish to picture yourself standing in a gentle, cool breeze after a hard sweat.) Silently begin repeating, "My forehead is cool. My forehead is cool." Continue repeating these self-suggestions for the entire seven- to ten-minute period.

DAY 7: You are to produce all six of the feelings, each for approximately two minutes. Silently begin repeating each of the following self-suggestions for a two-minute period.

1. I am feeling heavier and heavier.
2. I am feeling warmth throughout my body.
3. My heartbeat is regular and slow.
4. My breathing is slow, relaxed, and calm.
5. My stomach is warm, relaxed, and calm.
6. My forehead is cool.

Things to remember:

- Repeat all the self-suggestions slowly and intently—you want them to stick in your mind.
- Whenever possible, combine the suggestions with vivid imagination.

After completing this seven-day autogenic training program, you are to repeat the entire sequence for one more week. By practicing these techniques, you can quickly enter an "autogenic state" by simply repeating a suggestion like, "My hands and arms are heavy." This represents an important step in establishing the "mental triggers" for performance that will lead to decreased arousal levels.

MEDITATION AS A MENTAL TOUGHNESS TRAINING STRATEGY

Many top-performing athletes, like Billie Jean King, Joe Namath, and Bill Walton, have endorsed meditation as a valuable psychological training technique. Meditation improves one's ability to relax and to focus, and it's also a powerful source of positive energy. For centuries mystics have reported that the practice of meditation leads to the development of an inner peace, serenity, and joy that can be obtained in no other way. This inner harmony and peace, they report, in addition to renewing one's zest for life, establishes the kind of internal conditions that result in the *freeing* of human potential and talent.

According to Zen teachings, during meditation, the mind is fully alert and brilliantly clear. It is in a state of total attention and vivid awareness combined with a genuine feeling of joy. The final stage of Zen is "no-mind," or pure spontaneity in all acts. This state reportedly brings simplicity, spontaneity, and effortless grace with the full awareness of the here and now. All self-consciousness is lost in the act of focusing.

What is perhaps most interesting about this description of meditation is that it sounds remarkably similar to the description that athletes give when they are performing at their peaks. The mental state appears very similar—alert, spontaneous, fully aware, no self-consciousness. It is a perfect description of the ideal mental state for performing activities.

Important Understandings

The use of meditation as a mental training technique for sports requires that you understand the following concepts:

- Meditation represents a form of *concentration* practice. It is attentional retraining leading toward *attentional fitness.*
- The practitioner of meditation initially is surprised to find

how *attentionally* spastic he is. Dedicated practice enables you to move from mindlessness (attentionally spastic) to mindfulness (totally focused and aware without any self-consciousness).

- Most meditation methods utilize a mental focusing technique.
- The mental state to be achieved through meditation is characterized by alertness, not dullness or sleepiness.
- In addition to teaching attention control, meditation techniques teach profound relaxation.
- The meditative state is best described as a combination of high positive energy (joy), profound mental calmness, alertness, and deep physical relaxation of the muscles.
- You do not need to subscribe to any philosophical or religious belief system for the techniques to be effective.

Selected Meditation Techniques

Your meditation practice should be conducted where you won't be disturbed. For the best results, sit quietly in a comfortable position. Meditating when you are sleepy is difficult, so select a time when you are not likely to fall asleep. Initial practice sessions should last ten to fifteen minutes. Best results are obtained with two sessions each day.

1. Breath-Counting Meditation.

    Your *mental target* is your breath. Using the deep breathing method described in an earlier chapter, count your breaths from one to four. Silently say the number to yourself as you slowly exhale. When you reach four, start with one again. If your attention drifts, and this is common at the beginning, return to the count of one and continue forward again. For the best results, keep your eyes closed. When you master the four count, you may move to progressively higher numbers.

2. Object Meditation

    Your *mental target* is any object of your choice. Clear your mind for one object of deep concentration. This practice can be done with your eyes open and fixed on the object or with your eyes closed, imagining the object. The purpose is to maintain your concentration on the object for the length of time of the meditation. Should your attention shift, simply bring it back to the object again.

3. Mantra Meditation

Your *mental target* is any word of your choice. The word "one" is a commonly used mantra, but you may select another word if you wish. Repeat the word "one" in rhythm with your breathing. Pronounce it silently and slowly in conjunction with your process of exhaling. Focus all your attention on your mantra (your word). When you find your thoughts wandering, gently refocus on the mantra.

4. Eating or Walking Meditation

Your *mental target* is either your eating or your walking. During an eating meditation you are to focus your total attention on the process of eating; become totally mindful of eating. If your attention drifts, gently return it to your eating. The same holds for a walking meditation. Your full awareness should be turned toward your walking.

This kind of meditation can be practiced for any common, everyday activity. The goal is to become "utterly mindful," to fully focus as you act. The skill you develop from this kind of practice relates directly to your skill in controlling your attention during competitive play.

Meditation Requires Patience

Meditation is a technique that, with work and self-discipline, takes you to a special state of consciousness. It includes direct practice of elements of the Ideal Performance State. As you begin your meditation efforts, you may be surprised to find how undisciplined and difficult to control your mind is. This technique, initially, is a difficult one, and results do not occur suddenly. You will find, however, that practice and discipline will bring definite and definable results. So, if you "just can't seem to get it," endure the difficult period. STAY WITH IT!

BREATH CONTROL TRAINING

You may not be aware of it, but your breathing plays an important role in controlling and regulating your Ideal Performance State during play. The pattern of your breathing is different when you are relaxed and calm than when you are tense, anxious, or negative. Short, jerky, shallow, and irregular breaths usually accompany states of high negative arousal. Maintaining balance between excitement and relaxation is directly related to your skill in controlling your breathing patterns.

Learning this control begins by increasing your awareness of how you breathe when performing well. Contrast that with your breathing patterns when you are performing poorly. You will probably note a major difference. If you are like most players, when you are relaxed and playing well, your breathing is rhythmic, deep, and free.

Through biofeedback, we have learned that inhaling causes muscle tension to increase and holding your breath causes muscle tension to initially remain constant and then gradually increase. Breathing out, however, causes muscle tension to decrease. This is why experienced athletes have instinctively learned to coordinate their out-breath with critical points of execution, such as shooting the puck in hockey; serving in tennis; striking, blocking, or throwing in the martial arts; lifting in power weight lifting; carving a difficult turn in downhill racing; shooting a basketball, and so on. To insure this, many players develop a grunt as they execute.

When your biological alarm is triggered, your normal pattern of breathing changes. You begin to hold your breath or even inhale as you release the ball, shoot the puck, or lift at the critical point. This seemingly minimal change can result in dramatic drops in performance. Breathing is typically an automatic and spontaneous operation. However, *you can intervene and take direct voluntary control of your breathing when things go badly.*

Breath Control Strategies During Play

1. When performing well, don't think about or be concerned with your breathing.
2. When feeling emotionally flat or lifeless, speed your breathing up until you feel higher energy and activation levels.
3. When negative energy is flowing and you're racing too fast inside, slow your breathing way down. Take deep, long, and regular breaths whenever possible.
4. Attempt to coordinate the process of exhaling with critical moments of execution.

5. Select a word like "easy" or "power" or "yes" and slowly pronounce it as you execute the critical point of movement. This insures that you will properly exhale as you perform.

Breath Control Strategies Off the Athletic Field

With practice, you can acquire considerable skill in regulating your breathing. According to Eastern teachings, the control and regulation of your breathing is essential in learning appropriate control over your body and for achieving the kind of body awareness that ultimately leads to self-fulfillment.

The recommended breathing technique that has proved most effective within the realm of athletics follows.

STEP 1: Inhale slowly, continuously, and deeply through your nostrils, to a count of four. Relax—don't strain. Let the steady flow of incoming air fill and expand the central part of your body, including the lower abdomen as well as the central and upper chest cavity. Your stomach and lower abdomen should be fully pushed outward during this inhalation process. Practice this a couple of times, roughly to a count of four.

STEP 2: Momentarily pause before exhaling.

STEP 3: Exhale slowly and continuously through the mouth. As you do this, a distinctive sound will be heard—the sound of ahhhhhhhhhh. The sound should also be clear, continuous, and long. The exhalation process should last roughly to a count of ten. Practice a couple of times, making the sound of ahhhhhhhhhh, before putting the breathing method all together.

Your normal rate of breathing is about fourteen to sixteen breaths a minute. With this technique, you reduce it to as few as four and sometimes three, and feel very comfortable. When under pressure, you can slow down and return arousal levels to an acceptable range with three or four deep, prolonged breaths.

Summary

The importance of proper breathing to peak performance cannot be overemphasized. Breathing is normally an automatic and spontaneous process; however, anger, fear, or anxiety can disturb its natural rhythm and flow. When this happens, you can do two things.

First, recognize that your normal pattern of breathing has changed. Second, understand that you can control the process of your breathing when the situation calls for it.

Breath control practice off the athletic field can substantially aid your efforts to control and regulate your breathing on the field. The breathing technique presented in this chapter is such a training exercise. Obviously, it is not to be used during play, but the effects of this practice will naturally occur as you perform.

Begin your training efforts by monitoring your breathing during play and practice, becoming aware of how it changes under pressure. Become aware of how you breathe when you are performing exceptionally well. Do you typically hold your breath, inhale, or exhale as you execute? If you're not sure, experiment and find out.

Remember: if you're playing well, don't think about your breathing—leave the process on automatic.

Activation Training

The Art of Getting Energized

Being under-energized and working at a low energy level is sometimes a problem for athletes. The remedy for that is a skill called ACTIVATION.

Let's briefly look at some typical signs of under-activation associated with a poor performance.

- Feeling as if you don't have much energy or fire.
- Feeling of being slow—like a cold-starting engine.
- Poor concentration—easily distracted.
- Low patience and "don't really care" feeling.
- Noticeable absence of enthusiasm or excitement.
- Poor sense of timing or anticipation—frequently *late* timing.
- Physically look bored or lazy.
- A sense of helplessness ("nothing I do works").

The more quickly you can recognize your lowered energy level during play, the better are your chances of responding before it's too late. Once you've determined that you're not energized enough to play well, the following strategies should prove helpful *during play*:

1. Increase your breathing rate. Take short, quick breaths until you feel your arousal level increase.
2. Jump up and down on your toes. Get your body moving as much as possible to improve circulation and increase heart rate, blood pressure, etc.
3. Think challenging thoughts and ideas. Remember, thinking certain thoughts can produce tremendous energy. You should identify which thoughts are powerful triggers of emotion and energy for you. They may be thoughts of pride, personal excellence, the ecstasy of winning, the self-challenge, or whatever.
4. Mentally review very quickly your most important goals and objectives as an athlete. Why are you out there playing? That alone may raise your energy level enough to substantially improve your performance.
5. Verbally tell yourself things like, "I can do it"; "Let's get going"; "I can and will play well"; "My energy level is rising."
6. Alternate contracting and relaxing your muscles.
7. Create the strongest mental image that you can of yourself playing "in your finest hour." Recapture "the feeling."
8. Even though you don't feel energized or psyched, start acting "as if" you do. You can often change how you feel inside, which is the essence of activation, by simply acting "as if" you really do feel that way.
9. Always give your best effort no matter how energized you feel. Sometimes the right energy-producing feelings don't come. When that happens, it's guts and determination that carry you through.

Doing Your Homework Before You Perform

You can decrease your chances of encountering significant under-activation problems during a performance if you work to get things right *before* you perform. When you feel right, you tend to be energized right. The right feelings and emotions automatically produce appropriate activation. For most athletes, getting psyched for play is the same as getting the right feelings. "Those winning feelings" rep-

Year after year, the remarkable genius of Nolan Ryan's fastball finds expression. His special talent consistently surfaces because he has worked hard to acquire exceptional mental poise, emotional control, and self-confidence.

resent your best insurance, not only against under-activation problems, but other performance problems as well.

CENTERING AND DYNAMIC ENERGY

Wisdom from the Past

Much can be learned about the devastating effects of tension and ways to control it by examining the rich history of the martial arts. The legendary Japanese Samurai warrior had to be prepared to face death every day. How did he overcome the effects of fear and tension in combat? His very survival was intimately tied to his ability to conquer fear, self-consciousness, and self-doubt. The edict was simple: develop the proper mental control and attitude or die.

The effects of excessive tension were well understood. Fear and tension seriously undermined the warrior's ability to react powerfully and accurately, restricting his balance, perception, and judgment.

Teachers constantly searched for new methods of teaching and developing the necessary mental disposition and control, which were considered even more essential than physical techniques and skill. Inner self-control, which enabled the warrior to sustain an essential calm, clarity, and balance, was considered the single most important element in successful combat. The history of the martial arts reveals the overwhelming importance of *Mental Training* and the dedicated search by teachers to discover new methods of teaching these mental skills.

Two concepts dealing with the learning of proper mental control consistently reappeared over the centuries and eventually achieved nearly universal acceptance as the cornerstones to proper mastery. These are the concepts "Center" and "Dynamic Energy."

Centering

Philosophically, total man can be viewed as the perfect balance of the physical, mental, and spiritual. Man's world, however, is confusing, chaotic, and perplexing. Fulfillment requires that he find a basic harmony with himself and the world around him. This harmony represents a balance, a balance that brings calm, openness, fulfillment, and clarity. This point of balance and harmony is called the center or "one point." Commonly referred to by the Japanese word "hara," the concept of center can be helpful to performing athletes.

Being centered can be compared to our Western understanding of a person's "center of gravity." It is that point where you achieve maximum balance relative to your weight and height. In Eastern thought, this balance point is more than the point at which maximum physical balance is achieved. It represents an essential training concept whereby total balance, harmony, and unity of mind and body can be realized. *Being centered is a prerequisite for freeing and coordinating the full range of your potentials and powers.*

This point or spot of maximum coordination is located in the lower abdomen (roughly two inches below your navel). Maintaining your "one point," then, requires the development of a new point of reference. Being tense, fearful, self-conscious, rigid, and emotional are opposite to being *centered*.

Being centered brings balance and stability, poise and readiness, relaxed suppleness, intense awareness, total concentration, and clarity of vision. The loss of centeredness for the Samurai warrior during combat meant death. Maintaining that single spot in the lower abdomen became synonymous with the life and death struggle itself.

Once the center was lost, fear and tension would immediately lead to muscle rigidity, loss of quickness and agility, impairment of vision, loss of concentration, and, ultimately, failure! Becoming focused and centered on the *one spot* provided the warrior with a concrete method of conquering fear, tension, and anxiety. It became the vehicle for responding positively and confidently, even when confronted with the ultimate contest—the contest of life and death.

The principal methods for acquiring centering and concentration skills were meditation and systematic breathing practice. In meditation exercises, maintenance of the single spot in the lower abdomen became the center of focus. Maintenance of that spot during turbulent times such as combat was also closely tied to the ability to successfully regulate the breathing process.

Dynamic Energy

An important consequence of being centered, according to Eastern tradition and the martial arts, is that a new source of dynamic energy becomes available. This centered energy, called Ki by the Japanese, represents a powerful force in realizing human potential. It is much more than just the physical energy required to activate the muscular system.

"Ki" enables man to extend beyond his ordinary limits and transcend the boundaries of everyday living. It is the dynamic energy leading to genius, personal excellence, and fulfillment. The centralized energy of "Ki" makes possible the full realization of human powers and potentials. This energy is present in all human beings but exists in an ununified, sporadic, and dispersed form.

As centering occurs, this energy is focused, coordinated, and funneled, transforming it into a dynamic, positive force. The concept of center (hara) and energy (Ki) are, therefore, bound together. No center—no Ki. According to ancient teachings, the techniques for learning how to unleash this energy center on meditation, concentration, and breathing exercises.

Centering, Dynamic Energy, and the Athlete

Oscar Ratti and Adela Westbrook, noted authors of *Secrets of the Samurai,* thoroughly reviewed the training exercises used in ancient Japan for learning mastery of a number of martial arts including archery, swordsmanship, wrestling, jujitsu, judo, karate, and Aikido. In all cases, mastery of the technique involved not only learning a set of fundamental physical skills, but more importantly, learning the proper mental attitude and mental control which would accompany those physical skills.

In the art of archery, meditation and abdominal centralization were customarily practiced, as this training enabled the warrior to stand calmly and concentrate fully, even in battle. Abdominal breathing and meditation were also considered essential practices in proper mastery of the art of swordplay in feudal Japan. Just as the body had to be exercised, so did the mind.

When the mind becomes distracted by the circumstances of combat, all is lost. The mind must be trained to see everything and be distracted by nothing. It must maintain an intense and full awareness accompanied by an unshatterable calm. The mental exercises and training freed the warrior from the most devastating obstacle to his own survival—the paralyzing effects of tension and fear.

In wrestling and all forms of unarmed combat, mental development is consistently considered critical for mastery. The historical message, therefore, is clear: meditation and systematic breathing exercises are

In becoming the 1976 Olympics' Decathalon champion, Bruce Jenner described a very strange but powerful feeling that came over him during competition. He began to feel like there was nothing he couldn't do if he had to. He experienced an awesome and joyous sense of power that propelled him well beyond his own best times.

of great value in overcoming the effects of tension and fear and for freeing a positive source of dynamic energy.

Today's athlete is confronted with a similar but less dramatic dilemma. He is faced with the challenge of controlling the effects of tension. He is faced with similar problems of concentration, fear of failure, and self-consciousness. If the *ultimate* test of a technique's effectiveness is in a life-and-death struggle, then we can learn from those feudal warriors. Their strict adherence to mental-conditioning and training techniques presents a convincing picture.

The concepts of centering (hara) and centralized power and energy (Ki) can have great meaning to today's athlete. Meditation and systematic breathing exercises are methods that can significantly help an athlete's quest for excellence. And excellence comes from the *conquest of self*.

THE PERFORMANCE SLUMP

Causes and Cures

"I've been playing so well for the last five months, and then, all of a sudden, everything fell apart. I can't seem to get it back."

"The injury is over now but I can't seem to get my old form back. I'm 100 percent physically, but definitely not playing like it. I can't figure out what's the matter."

"I guess I've reached my peak. I haven't seen any improvement in a year."

"I'm working harder than ever, putting in more time than ever, and there's absolutely no progress."

"I'm about ready to quit. I'm sick and tired of playing so poorly!"

Do any of these sound familiar? Every serious athlete has probably made similar comments. The experience of peaks and valleys in performance seems to be inevitable. The question is "Why?" "Why can I play so well for a period of time and then suddenly stop, for no apparent reason? Is it something that goes wrong with my head? I don't feel any different. What causes these drops in performance that can last anywhere from one to two weeks to several months? Can anything be done about them?"

The initial causes of performance slumps often fall into the following five categories:

1. New changes in physical skills.
2. Natural learning plateaus.
3. Physical changes.
4. Mental changes.
5. Increased awareness.

1. *New Changes in Physical Skills.*

Do you know that your overall level of play will likely take a *drop* immediately following a change or modification in your form or technique? This occurence is particularly common when the new learning involves major changes in existing habits. This often shocks athletes who expect immediate improvement.

What happens? The new learning establishes a network of competing responses that often results in an inefficient mixture of the old with the new. The initial change in form or technique may feel great at the time, but with pressure, the older and more dominant habits will reappear, often producing an unworkable and uncontrollable mixture. Top athletes are reluctant to introduce significant modifications in form or technique during a competitive season in which they want to do well. *New learning can often have the effect of producing a temporary performance slump.*

In such cases, however, performance should steadily improve with regular drill and practice. Discontinuation of competitive play during this critical relearning phase generally increases the speed of learning and reduces the level of frustration.

Improving your form and technique usually enables you to move to higher levels of performance—but not immediately.

2. *Natural Learning Plateaus.*

Unfortunately, the mastery of complex physical skills rarely follows a steady, continuous pattern. Periods frequently occur where no observable progress is apparent, in spite of diligent practice and hard work. These often agonizing periods of learning are referred to as PLATEAUS and seem to follow no predictable pattern. We assume that necessary learning is taking place during these times, but is not directly observable in performance. Plateaus can also be viewed as a necessary incubation or gestation period for new learning. They appear to be an inevitable by-product of fine motor skill learning. The important consideration here is that *learning plateaus can initially contribute to the occurrence of performance slumps.*

3. *Physical Changes*

As discussed in a previous chapter, the occurrence of physical cycles has a bearing on overall level of play. Although these physical low periods do not generally lead to a long-standing performance slump, in combination with other factors, such as self-confidence drops, they can be contributing factors.

Physical injuries of one sort or another are often associated with the onset of a performance slump. The slump initially has a physical cause, but if it persists after the injury is healed, the cause has become psychological.

Other physical factors, such as extended fatigue, health problems, and poor diet, are associated with persistent performance problems.

4. *Mental Changes*

As you might expect, persistent performance slumps are often psychological in nature. A physical injury or a natural learning plateau may have triggered an initial drop in performance, but the persistence of the slump may be entirely due to mental factors. Low self-confidence, negative attitudes, increased tension, and arousal contribute to what is commonly referred to as a "negative spiral." In cases such as this, a complete recycling is needed. As new perspectives, new attitudes, and new expectations are born, the performance slump seems to vanish.

5. *Increased Awareness*

Just as the introduction of new learnings in the physical realm can result in temporary disruptions in performance, new learnings in the mental realm can have similar effects. The primary difference is that the disruptions are much less frequent and generally of considerably shorter duration. As you increase your awareness of muscle tension levels, energy states, breathing patterns, negative attitudes, etc., your customary mental responses are changed. Because of this, for a brief time you may find it difficult to perform spontaneously and automatically. If this does occur, it is typically short-lived. Many athletes do not experience any disruption and are able to integrate the new learning almost immediately into play. If disruption does occur, leading to a genuine performance slump, it is due to other contributing factors.

Recommended Training Strategies (For Eliminating Stubborn Performance Slumps):

Take a careful look at your physical health. Is your physical body capable of *maximum performance?* This includes noting injuries of any kind, persistent colds or infections, etc. Are you on any new medication or drugs? Have any significant changes occurred in your eating, sleeping, or drinking habits? What are the chances that the performance slump is related to *physical factors?* If significant physical factors are identified, those must be dealt with first. Until you are physically healthy, maximum performance *cannot occur*, no matter how mentally tough you are.

In your judgment, if physical factors do not represent major contributors to the performance slump now, assume the slump is due to *mental factors*.

The initial onset of the slump may have been associated with injuries or ill health, but if these no longer exist, the primary problems are now psychological. When psychological or mental factors are largely responsible for the slump, the following steps are recommended:

STEP 1: Acknowledge and accept the fact that your slump is resulting from your current attitudes, beliefs, mind sets, and confidence levels. Slumps have the effect of dramatically disrupting arousal levels, of lowering frustration levels, and of intensifying feelings of worthlessness and guilt. What is important here is that you commit yourself to a *psychological recycling effort.*

STEP 2: If possible, take a break from your normal training schedule, even if it is just a day or two. This can be very helpful in beginning to break the "negative spiral."

STEP 3: Make a conscious and deliberate effort each day to have fun with your sport and to renew your enthusiasm and excitement for playing. Review your personal goals and objectives. To break through the slump, you need a renewed sense of motivation which translates into High Positive Energy.

STEP 4: Increase your level of physical conditioning. Remember, physically stronger means mentally tougher.

STEP 5: Spend ten to fifteen minutes twice daily reconstructing attitudes, beliefs, and thoughts. Begin each session with five to seven minutes of relaxation, followed by visualization and imagery practice. Visualize yourself breaking through to new, exciting levels of performance. "See" and "feel" your self-confidence grow. Reprogram your inner world of experience as vividly and realistically as possible. Repeat several times to yourself, "I am breaking through; I am breaking through." Practice recapturing those "winning feelings."

STEP 6: Don't try to force it! Take the pressure off. Let the breakthrough occur naturally. And it *will* when the internal conditions are right.

PREPARING FOR THE BIG GAME

The Do's and Don't's

If you can play well and win the next two games, you'll make the playoffs for the first time ever. The whole season boils down to these last two games over the next two weeks. You want to make the playoffs more than anything, and you can feel the pressure mounting. What can you do to ensure your best performance in important games such as these? How should you prepare?

Do

Maintain your regular physical training program. Do your ordinary running, rope-jumping, speed and agility drills, and whatever else you customarily do. Remember, the relationship between physical strength and endurance and mental strength and endurance is real. Stay on the schedule of eating, sleeping, drinking, practicing, and playing that has proved best for you in the past. Exercise good self-discipline in your training before important events. Self-discipline is an excellent self-confidence builder.

Don't

Don't significantly change the physical training routine that has worked best in the past. Adding a good deal more exercise such as running or weight lifting at this point will probably interfere with your efforts to play well in the big game. This is not a time for *over-training*. You want to stay in good physical shape, but significantly changing your habits now will likely result in muscle soreness, stiffness, and perhaps even injury. Don't break your training routine before important games if at all possible.

Do

Spend a little time each day thinking and rehearsing how you want to perform for the big game. It may be for only a few minutes each day, but this is a particularly important part of being mentally prepared when the big day comes.

Don't

Don't wait until the night before to do all your mental preparation. No last minute cramming of information! Such a practice generally leads to confused play. Too much information at the last minute overload the circuit. Mentally prepare a little each day.

Do

Prepare yourself mentally and physically for anything that might happen during the big game. Remember the dictum: never be surprised by anything! An athlete who is surprised is in trouble. It's not that you expect bad things to happen; it simply means you're prepared if they do. In other words, you don't panic and can respond intelligently.

Don't

Don't make any major changes in your physical skills at this time. Go with what you've got. Introducing major changes in batting techniques, throwing, etc., is likely to be disruptive at this time. To play to your best, you need to be able to turn-on-the-automatic, and this is generally not possible with newly acquired physical skills.

Do

Do everything you can to achieve a physical, emotional, and intellectual high for the game. Avoid things that are likely to get you particularly tired, depressed, sad, upset, or negative.

In most any top-ten list of mentally tough athletes, Larry Bird's name would certainly appear. Perhaps the most remarkable aspect of his brilliant career has been his ability to summon his talents when his team needed them most. Bird has clearly learned how to transform pressure into challenge.

Don't

Don't get involved in activities, events, or situations that are likely to lead to personal problems or major conflicts. Major conflicts in your personal life often leave you physically and emotionally drained. Such conflicts are often responsible for emotionally "flat" and uninspired play. This is a particularly important consideration on the day of the game. Avoid fights, horror movies, catastrophic news, upsetting relationships, etc. These undermine positive energy flow and often lead to premature fatigue and tiredness. Staying alert, positive, energized, and focused during play may be impossible when you are emotionally spent.

Do

Start building momentum within yourself both during and away from practice. In other words, get the positive energy flowing. Every chance you get, attempt to stimulate increased team spirit, positiveness, enthusiasm, eagerness, and confidence. Stimulate an avalanche of positive energy for yourself and the team.

Don't

Don't get anxious about being anxious. It is perfectly natural and normal to be nervous. Worrying about worrying just makes the situation worse. Some pre-game nervousness is unavoidable and may simply be an indication that you're really "psyched" to play well. The same general attitude should be taken with sleep as well. Don't worry about not sleeping the night before the big game. Research shows that a restless night of sleep the night before a game will usually not hurt performance—*if you don't worry about it!*

Do

Dress to win. If your blue socks are the winning ones, wear them. If you have to put your right shoe on first to be lucky, do it! The point is that you should do whatever helps you to get "those winning feelings." Superstition or not, if it helps, do it. These are called *dress rituals,* and they are important.

Don't

Don't eat anything substantial within two hours of the game. You should *rigidly* follow your best routine for food and beverage intake before play.

Do

Most importantly, have fun and enjoy yourself during the big game. This will help to furnish energy and also keep you relaxed during play. Rehearse the habits of thought during the week that are important to your play. They include:

- I will give 100 percent effort, no matter what.
- I will stay positive and optimistic.
- I will stay calm, relaxed, and confident during play.
- I will perform well.

Practice visualizing each day how you want to perform and how you want the team to perform on the day of the big game. See it happen in your mind first!

BUILDING TEAM HARMONY

The ingredients of team spirit are mutual respect, good communication, closeness, trust, acceptance, and encouragement. Any number of things can happen that tend to undermine team spirit. Sometimes a player may feel shut out or rejected by his teammates. He may develop feelings of resentment or anger at the coach for something he said or did. Players occasionally may feel some degree of isolation from others on a team, may feel unappreciated or unaccepted, or may not get along well with certain members of a team. When things like this happen, both team and individual performance levels generally drop. It is very important, therefore, that you understand the relationship between peak performance and team harmony, and that you take the necessary steps to ensure the highest level of team unity that you can.

Just as every athlete has an Ideal Performance State, so does every team. The realization of a team's IPS is directly related to the quality of interaction among its members. The study of Olympic athletes has demonstrated a strong link between team unity and team accomplishment. As we have already seen, team spirit is a powerful source of positive energy, and when it's there, every player seems to come alive. Athletes report that team spirit not only keeps them feeling pumped up and energized but also takes the pressure off. Players feel more relaxed, give more of themselves, and play more confidently when an atmosphere of team unity and togetherness is present.

It sounds strange, but most successful coaches will tell you that the performance potential of a team as a unit is much greater than the addition of each player's level of talent individually. Have you ever played on a team where, although most agreed there wasn't a great deal of talent, you accomplished some pretty amazing things? When that happens, and it often does, one thing is certain—team spirit and unity were high. The presence of team spirit draws people out and makes them feel a part of something much bigger than themselves. It also encourages players to take risks and to extend themselves beyond their normal limits. It breeds inspiration, confidence, and intensity. In short, team spirit makes the realization of every player's Ideal Performance State seem easy and automatic.

The True Test Is Adversity

The quickest way to determine the depth of team unity is to observe what happens in adverse situations. One of two things usually happens. Players either withdraw into themselves, or they turn to the group to cope with the increased pressure. When the mutual support system of the team is not sufficiently developed, players' typical coping strategy is to withdraw into themselves or to splinter off in groups of two or three.

In other words, adversity pulls team members apart rather than binding them closer together. The reason is that the trust and support for one another is not there. Often team members start playing for themselves; they start trying to turn the situation around on their own. The natural consequence is that players suddenly find themselves becoming overly emotional and negative and are quick to criticize. An increasing air of defensiveness develops, and individual team members, to avoid criticism, start playing not to make mistakes. Team play becomes, at best, tentative and uninspired, and at worst, confused and disoriented.

When the support system is strong enough, however, players instinctively pull together in adversity. They find the security they need by moving closer toward the group, not further away. The players tend to see the crisis as a threat to the team itself and not so much to themselves personally. Support and encouragement for one another spontaneously starts to increase as the crisis intensifies. Players feel a strong urge to avoid criticism or negativism toward one another. In sharp contrast to the withdrawal strategy, the enemy is clearly seen as coming from the outside—not the inside.

How Does It Happen

Coming together as a team is directly related to three primary factors. The first is time. Building a stable mutual support system is a very complicated process and therefore takes time. The more time individuals have to spend together, the greater the likelihood that a stable mutual support system will naturally develop. It doesn't happen overnight. The process can be accelerated by doing certain things, but there is no adequate substitute for time together.

The second factor to be considered is the number of changes each person must adjust to. Change creates instability, and instability breeds suspicion, distrust, and confusion. The more new faces, new positions, new policies, new coaches, new styles, etc., the longer the team building process will be extended.

The third important factor concerning the team building process is the interaction of the personalities involved. Some players are more open and trusting than others. Some are quick to criticize and become defensive while others are not. The interaction of the coach's personality with that of his players and the players with each other is fundamentally important. Unfortunately, distrust, defensiveness, and negativism are highly contagious on a team, particularly in the early stages of team building. Players and coaches alike must work doubly hard during this time to eliminate the negatives. Once negative energy gets started, it's tough to shut it down.

Positive Peer Pressure—The Telltale Sign

When I am trying to determine how much team unity has developed on a team, I always look at one factor—*peer pressure*. It's the single best indicator I've found thus far. A poor mutual support system forces players into the situation of not wanting to make mistakes because they fear criticism from their teammates, coaches, or fans.

A strong support system, on the other hand, involves an entirely different kind of incentive, an incentive that takes the form of, "I don't want to let the guys down." This type of peer pressure has a dramatically positive impact on performance. Teammates end up playing *for each other* rather than for themselves. They are no longer playing to avoid criticism or punishment.

When this kind of peer pressure is present, adherence to team rules, team discipline, schedules, and giving 100 percent in play and practice is assured. Positive peer pressure is infinitely more powerful

Jim Plunkett is no stranger to adversity. From Heisman Trophy winner to the pits (Patriots, 49ers, and the Raiders) and then, when everyone counted him out, led his team to two Super Bowl titles. Jim was able to take charge and become a great leader because he was ready both physically and emotionally when the opportunity presented itself.

and constructive than pressure generated from coaches, parents, or fans.

Strategies for Building Team Harmony

1. Get to know your teammates.

   The more you understand about a person, the easier it is to accept his differences. It's easy to be critical and negative about a person you don't understand. Take time and listen to the person with whom you're having trouble. Try to see through his eyes. If you can do that, your feelings toward that person almost always improve.

2. Give positive feedback to your teammates whenever you get the chance.

   Simple statements like, "Good hustle," "Nice try," "Great job," "Super," or "I knew you could do it," help to build strong, positive relationships. Be positive and supportive verbally to your fellow players, and avoid the critical, negative feedback. In other words, get into the habit of saying things to your teammates that build them up, and avoid saying things that put them down. This is particularly true in adversity. Remember, everyone has the tendency to retreat into himself and protect number one when things get tough. When you're part of a team, that strategy spells trouble for you and everyone else. Work extra hard to be supportive, positive, and constructive with your team in adversity. By helping them, you end up helping yourself.

3. Give 100 percent effort in practice, and work hard on your weaknessses.

   Working hard to improve yourself and giving full effort is a powerful team unifier. When you are dedicated and committed, you encourage others to do likewise by example. Never underestimate the power of your example in building team spirit.

4. Both negativism and positivism are highly contagious.

   Don't be fooled into believing that your negative attitude isn't affecting your team. Negativism can spread through a team like a disease. Carefully guard what you *think* and *say*. Start an epidemic of enthusiasm and excitement on your team by being optimistic and positive.

5. Resolve conflicts with teammates or coaches as quickly as possible.

   Don't let conflicts build up inside. Take action to resolve them.

   Express your complaint or resolve your conflict with the person who is responsible for the situation and can alter it. Don't gripe or complain to others, venting your feelings—that just spreads negative energy. If you respond to a conflict responsibly and immediately, it will have little effect on your inner state and performance. But the longer it persists, the more you endanger your inner state and, hence, performance.

6. Get your attitude and disposition right *BEFORE* going to practice or games.

   Once you arrive for play, it's often too late to adjust your attitudes. The real pro *arrives* with the right frame of mind, ready to play his best.

7. Don't be a loudmouth or show-off.

   Neither one will produce many friends on a team. Quiet confidence, sincerity, and the ability to listen will serve you much better. The experience of team spirit is most generally described by players as the feeling of closeness between team members. Removing your facades and allowing others to know who and what you are is an important step in feeling close.

8. Go out of your way to help your teammates whenever you can.

   Being mutually interdependent on each other stimulates team spirit. When you help someone, they feel closer and more responsive to you.

9. Be fully responsible for yourself.

   Don't get into the habit of blaming others for your poor performances. Blaming the coach or your teammates when things don't go well for you serves no useful purpose. Work within positive and constructive channels to produce needed changes. Blaming only serves to frustrate team harmony building efforts.

10. Be your own best igniter.

    Don't rely on others to push you from behind to keep

you going. Self-starters are extremely valuable team members. They often become the triggers for positive momentum. Be a model of positive energy.

11. Communicate clearly, honestly, and openly with your coach.

To achieve a high level of team harmony, the communication between you and your coach must be healthy. The better you understand each other, the better your chances are of performing well.

12. Don't forget to have fun!

Being able to laugh and to loosen up a little often breaks down barriers and helps people to relax and feel closer. Remember, when you can enjoy, you can perform.

Chapter V
Assessing and Monitoring Your Mental Strengths and Weaknesses

Profiling Your Mental Skills

Increasing your awareness of your mental strengths and weaknesses is fundamental to accelerated change. The more you know and understand yourself and your limits, the better equipped you are to consistently perform toward the upper range of those limits. Improving self-understanding and self-awareness will help accelerate the mental strength learning process.

To help you sharpen your understanding of the dimension of mental toughness as it relates to your profile of strengths and weaknesses, I would like to examine seven separate mental skill areas. Although a much broader range of mental skills could be included, the seven areas listed below have consistently emerged as the most important and fundamental.

Self-Confidence
Your level of self-confidence is one of the best predictors of competitive success that we can point to. The feelings and images you have about what you can and can't do strongly determine the outcome. In many ways, maintaining high levels of self-confidence is a skill.

Top athletes are well aware that certain activities, people, thoughts, and images quickly undermine their confidence levels.

Self-confidence is a feeling and a knowing that says you can do it, that you can perform well and be successful. The key ingredient in self-confidence and self-belief is perceived success. Nothing can undermine confidence levels more quickly than an accumulation of perceived failures. Regardless of your level of physical talent and skill, if you have lost your confidence, your performance output will be dramatically affected.

Negative Energy

Controlling such negative emotions as fear, anger, frustration, envy, resentment, rage, and temper is essential to competitive success. Staying calm, relaxed, and focused is directly related to your ability to keep negative energy to a minimum. Negative energy control is tied to your ability to perceive difficult situations as challenges rather than as threats or frustrating problems. Fueling a performance from the negative emotions typically produces inconsistency, excessive muscle tension, and poor concentration. This is particularly true in fine motor skill sports such as golf and tennis.

Attention Control

The ability to sustain a continuous focus on the task at hand is so central to performing well that it cannot be overemphasized. Attention control is nothing more than the ability to "tune in" to what's important and "tune out" what's not. The goal is a one-pointed form of concentration, so complete that a total loss of "self" occurs in the act of focusing. The more deeply an athlete can become immersed in the relevant aspects of play, the deeper the concentration and the greater the loss of "self."

Athletes consistently report that they lose self-consciousness when they are concentrating well. This loss of self-consciousness, ironically, is accomplished by distraction, distracting attention away from the "self" by totally becoming the desired object of focus. The ability to achieve and maintain this kind of focus is learned and is linked directly to an athlete's skill in managing positive and negative energy flow.

Visualization and Imagery Control

Successful athletes invariably have well-developed visualization and imagery control skills. They are able to think in pictures rather than words, and they are able to control the flow of their mental pictures and images in positive and constructive directions. Performing well in sport requires that an athlete shift from a highly rational, logical, and deliberate style of thinking to a much more spontaneous, free-flowing, and instinctive one. Visualization and imagery practice both prior to and during performances helps to facilitate that shift.

Visualization is one of the most powerful mental training strategies thus far discovered for translating mental desires into physical performance. The key lies in the fact that the central nervous system is incapable of differentiating between a deeply rooted visualization and an actual physical event. Therefore, the more vivid, detailed, and real the visualization, the more powerful the effect. The ability to think in pictures rather than words, to control imagery flow in positive directions, and to visualize vividly and in great detail improves steadily with practice. This is a critical mental skill area in performance.

Motivation

Maintaining high levels of self-motivation is a skill. Setting meaningful goals, programming a steady diet of daily success, and managing failure properly are all critical components of motivation. They are also all learned. I cannot overemphasize the importance of self-motivation in performance. Motivation is ENERGY, and self-motivation is one of the most important sources of positive energy available to an athlete.

The willingness to persevere with training schedules and to endure the pain, discomfort, and self-sacrifice associated with the forward progress is linked to an athlete's level of self-motivation. Regardless of an athlete's physical skill level or talent, low self-motivation spells trouble. Of the seven variables, self-motivation is first in importance.

Positive Energy

Maintaining and controlling the flow of positive energy is an acquired skill. It is essentially the ability to become energized from such sources as fun, joy, determination, positiveness, and team spirit. Positive energy makes peak performance possible. It is the energy source that enables an athlete to achieve high levels of activation while simultaneously experiencing calmness, low muscle tension, and attentional control. It is closely related to motivational factors and attitude development.

Attitude Control

Attitude control simply reflects an athlete's habits of thought. The right attitudes produce emotional control, poise, and positive energy flow. Top performing athletes are disciplined thinkers. A specific constellation of attitudes characterize successful competitors. This dimension reflects the extent to which your personal attitudes are consistent with those of successful high-level performances.

Tim Mayotte reported that his competitive play moved to a whole new level of success after he followed the AET program as outlined in this book.

The Psychological Performance Inventory

To help you get a clearer idea of your mental strengths and weaknesses relative to the seven variables just reviewed, place an X in one of the five spaces for each of the items in the following list. Place only one check for each item. Your choices are ALMOST ALWAYS, OFTEN, SOMETIMES, SELDOM, and ALMOST NEVER. Select whichever one best fits your interpretation of the item as it relates to you in athletics. Your response is simply an estimate. Be as open and honest as you can with yourself and respond to each item as it pertains to you in the right-here-and-now context.

• Psychological Performance Inventory

1. I see myself as more of a loser than a winner in competition.

1	2	3	(4)	5
Almost Always	Often	Sometimes	Seldom	Almost Never

2. I get angry and frustrated during competition.

1	2	3	(4)	5
Almost Always	Often	Sometimes	Seldom	Almost Never

3. I become distracted and lose my focus during competition.

1	2	3	(4)	5
Almost Always	Often	Sometimes	Seldom	Almost Never

4. Before competition, I picture myself performing perfectly.

5	4	(3)	2	1
Almost Always	Often	Sometimes	Seldom	Almost Never

5. I am highly motivated to play my best.

(5)	4	3	2	1
Almost Always	Often	Sometimes	Seldom	Almost Never

6. I can keep strong positive emotion flowing during competition.

5	(4)	3	2	1
Almost Always	Often	Sometimes	Seldom	Almost Never

7. I am a positive thinker during competition.

5	④	3	2	1
Almost Always	Often	Sometimes	Seldom	Almost Never

8. I believe in myself as a player.

⑤	4	3	2	1
Almost Always	Often	Sometimes	Seldom	Almost Never

9. I get nervous or afraid in competition.

1	2	③	4	5
Almost Always	Often	Sometimes	Seldom	Almost Never

10. It seems my mind starts racing 100 mph during critical moments of competition.

1	2	3	4	⑤
Almost Always	Often	Sometimes	Seldom	Almost Never

11. I mentally practice my physical skills.

⑤	4	3	2	1
Almost Always	Often	Sometimes	Seldom	Almost Never

12. The goals I've set for myself as a player keep me working hard.

⑤	4	3	2	1
Almost Always	Often	Sometimes	Seldom	Almost Never

13. I am able to enjoy competition even when I face lots of difficult problems.

5	4	③	2	1
Almost Always	Often	Sometimes	Seldom	Almost Never

14. My self-talk during competition is negative.

1	2	3	④	5
Almost Always	Often	Sometimes	Seldom	Almost Never

15. I lose my confidence very quickly.

1	2	3	④	5
Almost Always	Often	Sometimes	Seldom	Almost Never

16. Mistakes get me feeling and thinking negatively.

1	2	③	4	5
Almost Always	Often	Sometimes	Seldom	Almost Never

17. I can clear interfering emotion quickly and regain my focus.

5	④	3	2	1
Almost Always	Often	Sometimes	Seldom	Almost Never

18. Thinking in pictures about my sport comes easy for me.

⑤	4	3	2	1
Almost Always	Often	Sometimes	Seldom	Almost Never

19. I don't have to be pushed to play or practice hard. I am my own best igniter.

⑤	4	3	2	1
Almost Always	Often	Sometimes	Seldom	Almost Never

20. I tend to get emotionally flat when things turn against me during play.

1	2	3	④	5
Almost Always	Often	Sometimes	Seldom	Almost Never

21. I give 100 percent effort during play, no matter what.

⑤	4	3	2	1
Almost Always	Often	Sometimes	Seldom	Almost Never

22. I can perform toward the upper range of my talent and skill.

5	4	③	2	1
Almost Always	Often	Sometimes	Seldom	Almost Never

23. My muscles become overly tight during competition.

1	2	3	4	⑤
Almost Always	Often	Sometimes	Seldom	Almost Never

24. I get spacey during competition.

1	2	3	4	⑤
Almost Always	Often	Sometimes	Seldom	Almost Never

25. I visualize working through tough situations prior to competition.

5	4	3	②_	1
Almost Always	Often	Sometimes	Seldom	Almost Never

26. I'm willing to give whatever it takes to reach my full potential as a player.

⑤	4	3	2	1
Almost Always	Often	Sometimes	Seldom	Almost Never

27. I practice with high positive intensity.

5	4	③	2	1
Almost Always	Often	Sometimes	Seldom	Almost Never

28. I can change negative moods into positive ones by controlling my thinking.

5	4	③	2	1
Almost Always	Often	Sometimes	Seldom	Almost Never

29. I'm a mentally tough competitor.

5	④	3	2	1
Almost Always	Often	Sometimes	Seldom	Almost Never

30. Uncontrollable events like the wind, cheating opponents, and bad referees get me very upset.

1	2	③	4	5
Almost Always	Often	Sometimes	Seldom	Almost Never

31. I find myself thinking of past mistakes or missed opportunities as I play.

1	2	3	④	5
Almost Always	Often	Sometimes	Seldom	Almost Never

32. I use images during play that help me perform better.

5	④	3	2	1
Almost Always	Often	Sometimes	Seldom	Almost Never

33. I get bored and burned out.

1	2	3	(4)	5
Almost Always	Often	Sometimes	Seldom	Almost Never

34. I get challenged and inspired in tough situations.

5	(4)	3	2	1
Almost Always	Often	Sometimes	Seldom	Almost Never

35. My coaches would say I have a good attitude.

5	(4)	3	2	1
Almost Always	Often	Sometimes	Seldom	Almost Never

36. I project the outward image of a confident fighter.

(5)	4	3	2	1
Almost Always	Often	Sometimes	Seldom	Almost Never

37. I can remain calm during competition when confused by problems.

5	(4)	3	2	1
Almost Always	Often	Sometimes	Seldom	Almost Never

38. My concentration is easily broken.

1	2	(3)	4	5
Almost Always	Often	Sometimes	Seldom	Almost Never

39. When I visualize myself playing, I can see and feel things vividly.

5	(4)	3	2	1
Almost Always	Often	Sometimes	Seldom	Almost Never

40. I wake up in the morning and am really excited about playing and practicing.

(5)	4	3	2	1
Almost Always	Often	Sometimes	Seldom	Almost Never

41. Playing this sport gives me a genuine sense of joy and fulfillment.

(5)	4	3	2	1
Almost Always	Often	Sometimes	Seldom	Almost Never

42. I can turn crisis into opportunity.

5	4	③	2	1
Almost Always	Often	Sometimes	Seldom	Almost Never

How to Score the Results

If you will go back and look, you will see a number beside each X you made for each item. For example:

Item   <u>X   5</u>

        Almost Always

Take that number and place it alongside the item number in the following chart, e.g., 6 <u>5</u> . After doing this for all 42 items, add each of the seven columns separately. Use that total for making your own profile of mental strengths and weaknesses. Any of your total scores which fall below 20 need your special attention. When that happens, thoroughly review all training procedures which relate to that area of weakness.

26–30 Excellent Skills
20–25 Room for Improvement
6–19 Needs Your Special Attention

Self-Confidence	Negative Energy	Attention Control	Visual & Imagery Control	Motiva-tional Level	Positive Energy	Attitude Control
1 _4_	2 _4_	3 _4_	4 _3_	5 _5_	6 _4_	7 _4_
8 _5_	9 _3_	10 _5_	11 _5_	12 _5_	13 _3_	14 _4_
15 _4_	16 _3_	17 _4_	18 _5_	19 _5_	20 _4_	21 _5_
22 _3_	23 _5_	24 _5_	25 _2_	26 _5_	27 _3_	28 _3_
29 _4_	30 _3_	31 _4_	32 _4_	33 _4_	34 _4_	35 _5_
36 _5_	37 _4_	38 _3_	39 _4_	40 _5_	41 _5_	42 _3_
25	22	25	23	29	23	24

FILL IN YOUR PROFILE

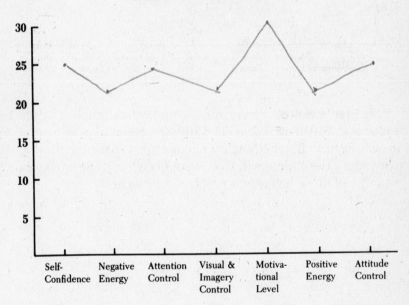

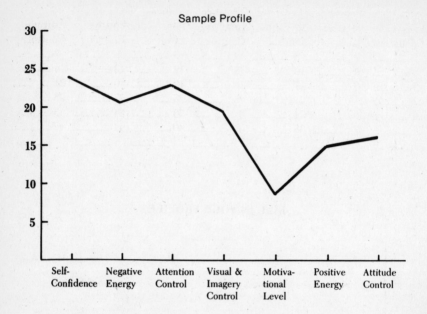

Sample Profile

This profile reflects a very serious motivation problem. Until this is changed, little is possible. The athlete's other areas of mental skill are satisfactory. If something isn't done to rectify the low level of self-motivation, the athlete will more than likely drop out or continue to be a discipline or behavioral problem for coaches.

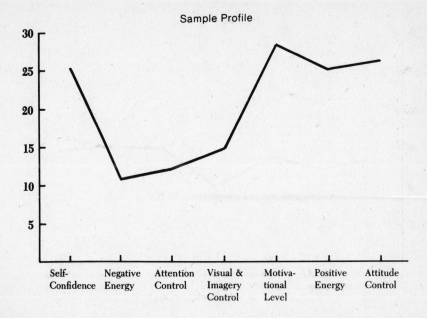

Sample Profile

This is a typical profile of a young athlete just getting into competitive sports. It represents a situation of considerable internal conflict. If something isn't done to improve this athlete's success in managing pressure, his motivation and self-confidence levels will soon start dropping. Players with profiles such as this rarely perform well competitively. Until their negative energy control skills improve, staying relaxed, calm, and focused in pressure situations is virtually impossible.

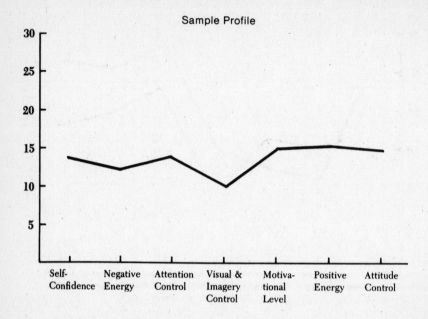

Although this profile indicates little conflict, performance output and forward progress will be minimal. For any substantial positive change in performance to occur, this athlete will have to risk a new level of involvement. Complacency is safe and, in all probability, this athlete has experienced considerable failure in his or her own eyes. Until the energy investment changes substantially, little is possible.

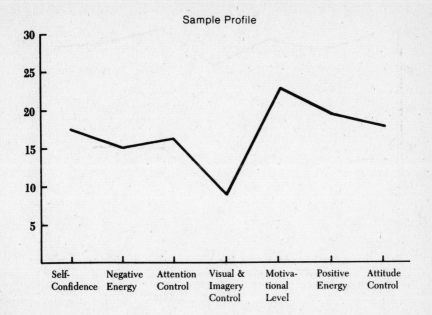

Sample Profile

This is again a rather typical profile. Many players are not aware of the importance of visualization and imagery skills, and therefore rarely practice or rehearse them. Improvement in visualizing and imagining automatically increases self-confidence, negative energy control, and attention control.

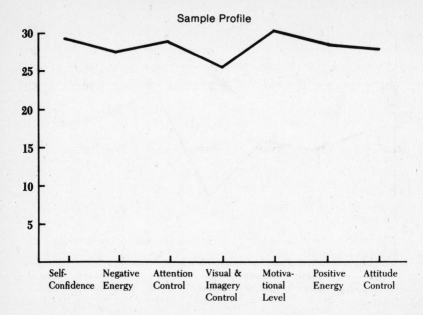

This is the profile of a champion. The high level of skills in all critical areas presents an impressive picture of mental strength. Highly successful performers reveal this kind of profile. Achieving a profile of strengths such as this is possible only through hard work, discipline, and effort. For some, the road is easier than for others, but nobody acquires these skill levels without a struggle—NOBODY!

There is nothing sacred or absolute about the pattern of your profile. It is one more tool you can use to potentially deepen your understanding, as a competitive athlete, of what you do well and what you do poorly from a psychological perspective. If it helps, use it. The more information you have about your strengths and weaknesses, the better.

You could obviously answer the questions so as to make yourself look stronger or weaker than you are. The intent of each item is quite clear, and consequently, distorting the final picture is possible. My experience has been, however, that athletes tend to be open and honest in their answers because they are genuinely interested in improving deficiencies.

The time at which you take the inventory also makes a difference. If you happen to be depressed or coming off a particularly tough loss, the results will be disproportionately low. Avoid taking the inventory during such times if possible.

As you study the results of your profile, take special note of any items scored with a one or two. This will help identify specific problem areas. If you're working hard to improve the mental weaknesses identified in your profile, take the inventory every so often, such as every six months, and see if positive changes are occurring. You'll be pleasantly surprised!

Strategies for Overcoming Deficiencies: A Final Summary

Low Self-Confidence
- **Increase your physical strength and endurance levels.**

  Initiate a rigorous physical conditioning program designed to increase strength and endurance. As you become physically stronger and more fit, you experience significant elevations in self-image and self-confidence.
- **Work hard to improve other mental skill deficiencies.**

  As you increase your ability to stay calm, relaxed, and focused during play, your self-confidence will steadily rise. As your mental skills in these areas improve, you start to *truly believe* that you do possess the kind of self-control necessary to perform well.
- **Set realistic self-goals.**

  You need success with yourself! Just as goal-setting helps to stimulate motivation, it also renews self-confidence. A steady diet of perceived success is not only the single most important element in staying self-motivated, it is also the most important ingredient in self-confidence.
- **Think positively and create enthusiasm.**

  What you believe about yourself is directly influenced by *what you think*. Pessimistic and negative thoughts and ideas erode your efforts to build high confidence levels. "We are what we think." If you program in negativism and self-defeatism, your confidence levels will reflect it.
- **Constantly repeat positive affirmations to yourself.**

  Listen to what you're telling yourself all day long. Too often, the dialogue we have with ourselves serves only to undermine our confidence. Comments like, "You'll never make it"; "You're going to choke"; "Dumb-head"; and "It's no use" are common. Start saying things like, "I can do it";

"I'm getting tougher"; "My confidence is growing"; and "I am a winner." These self-suggestions can substantially increase confidence levels.

- **Increase self-discipline.**

  As you exercise a higher degree of self-discipline in your training and practice, substantial increases in self-confidence levels are often realized. Again, self-discipline provides demonstrable evidence that "I am in control."

- **Use positive visualization.**

  "Seeing is believing." If you can see it happen in your imagination, you start believing. Practice seeing yourself being successful and achieving your objectives. The more you practice, the higher the confidence.

- **Review film of best performances.**

  If available, review film of prior performances which were notably successful. This alone can lead to sudden and oftentimes dramatic increases in confidence.

- **Act "as if."**

  Even if you don't feel self-confident, act "as if" you did. When you start behaving like you were confident, the feelings often start coming naturally.

- **Practice off the athletic field.**

  Practice triggering feelings of confidence at home. It's nothing more than a way of feeling, and you can come to control it with practice.

Low Negative Energy Control

- **Increase awareness.**

  The first step in improving control is to increase your awareness of what happens to you under pressure. When, where, how, and why does negative energy get triggered during play? What situations, thought patterns, and perceptions lead to threat? When and where do your muscles become overly tense and rigid? Under what circumstances are you likely to lose that all-important calmness and focus?

- **Breath control training.**

  The control and regulation of your breathing is fundamental to controlling energy levels. Taking deep and prolonged breaths, deliberately slowing down the overall breathing rate, and coordinating the process of exhaling with critical moments of execution can be a great help in establishing proper emotional balance. Practicing breath control is recommended both on and off the playing field.

• **Muscle relaxation training.**

Systematically tensing and relaxing various muscle groups of the body has proved to be a very helpful technique for reducing excessive muscle tension.

• **Autogenic training.**

This relaxation training technique focuses on the associative power of certain words to elicit a relaxation response and the power of self-suggestion. Repetition of phrases like, "I am feeling heavier," and, "My hands are feeling warmer and warmer," can produce profound relaxation effects. The power of words, the power of self-suggestion, and the power of one's imagination are emphasized. The autogenic model plays a central role in mental training procedures for athletes in European, and particularly Iron Curtain, countries.

• **Meditation training.**

Meditation can produce profound states of relaxation and reduce negative energy flow. Significant numbers of athletes have reported that various meditation techniques have been effective tension and anxiety-reducing strategies. A common technique is the repetition of a given word, such as the word "one," in coordination with exhalation. Others include focusing on the process of breathing or selecting and holding attention on a particular object. Any technique can be used, provided it results in the desired relaxation and quieting effects.

• **Thought control training.**

To achieve a high degree of self-control over negative energy flow, you *must* control what you are thinking. Focusing on disturbing and negative thoughts produces dramatically different arousal states than focusing on positive and constructive ones. Focusing on themes of winning and losing, missed opportunities, and self-condemnation only undermines your efforts.

• **Visualization and imagery rehearsal.**

Visualizing and imagining pleasant and relaxing scenes generally reduces negative energy levels and can, therefore, be used as a relaxation technique. Mentally rehearsing the desired physical and emotional responses to tension-producing situations can be very helpful.

• **Counter-conditioning strategies.**

Tension and anxiety reactions can become conditioned to various aspects of competitive play. These reactions can be tied to such things as the personality of the opponent, the place, the crowd, wind, or a particular aspect of play, such as hitting a backhand in tennis or a short putt in golf. Strategies to change this conditioning include sustaining a deeply relaxed response while at the same time maintaining a mental picture of the anxiety-producing situation. In effect, you are counter-conditioning a relaxation response to a situation that once produced anxiety and tension.

• **Self-hypnosis.**

Athletes frequently report that a combination of relaxation, self-suggestion, and imagery has been an effective method of controlling negative energy flow, particularly in the form of excessive muscle tension and anxiety.

• **Physical Exercise.**

Athletes who struggle with excessive muscle tension and anxiety levels during the early phases of a performance often find that mild physical exercise, such as jogging or bicycling, just prior to the event can be very helpful.

• **Create pressure situations during practice.**

The more you can simulate the pressure conditions that will be present during actual competitive play, the more opportunities you have to learn how to play as if there were no pressure. Practicing in pressure situations is one of the most effective strategies available for accelerating skills in relaxing, calming, and energy control during competitive play.

Low Attentional Control
• **Improve calming and quieting skills.**

Your ability to appropriately concentrate on the task at hand relates to your success in managing negative energy. Therefore, those techniques that assist you in managing anxiety and tension levels more effectively can be very helpful in improving your attention control skills. Excessive negative arousal usually leads to a dramatic narrowing of attention. Perception becomes fixated on inappropriate and irrelevant aspects of play, giving observers the impression that you are blind to the obvious. You may even appear "spaced out" or "out of touch" with what is happening. As negative arousal levels drop, this pattern quickly changes.

• **Meditation training.**

In addition to serving as a relaxation training technique, many meditation practices can serve as a form of concentration practice. Concentration is nothing more than focusing attention on a particular target and holding it there— "tuning in" what's relevant and "tuning out" what's irrelevant. A variety of meditation techniques involve this same activity.

• **Time awareness training.**

Playing well requires a "here-and-now" focus. By sharpening your awareness of whether you are performing in the "here-and-now"context or whether your focus is future- or past-oriented can be helpful. Consistently focusing on past or future events during play interferes with performance.

• **Centering strategies**

Taken essentially from the martial arts, centering involves establishing a state of perfect balance, both mentally and physically. To be centered, you must be focusing on what's relevant, exist in the "here-and-now" context, and be appropriately relaxed physically but intense and alert mentally. Being centered also requires a state of perfect physical balance. Prior to critical moments of execution, athletes have found it a very helpful concentration technique to check for centeredness.

• **Get the positive energy flowing.**

Any technique that helps to stimulate the flow of positive energy will automatically lead to increased attentional control. When you are properly energized and enjoying yourself, you automatically "tune in" to what's important.

• **Concentrate during practice.**

If you're having concentration problems during play, a concerted effort should be made to improve your concentration skills during practice. Work extra hard during your practices to sustain a continuous focus on what's important and block out what's not. You perform as you practice— both mentally and physically.

Low Visualization and Imagery Skills

- **Practice visualizing and imagining with all five senses.**

  Develop and sharpen your ability to create vivid mental pictures of places, events, and people THROUGH PRACTICE. The more you practice, the better you'll get. Make an effort to practice visualizing every day for a minimum of three to four minutes. Several short practice sessions are considerably more effective than one or two long ones.

- **Visualizing vividly requires internal calmness and quiet.**

  Visualization requires that you temporarily shut down the rational, logical, analytical you. Visualization by nature is non-logical and is produced in a distinctly different region of the brain than rational and logical thought. Calming and quieting help to make the neurological shift.

- **Use photographs, mirrors, or films**

  These can help strengthen and improve your ability to visualize yourself as a performer.

- **Review edited film.**

  The regular review of film where mistakes and errors have been edited out can have a powerful effect on building and strengthening positive and mechanically correct visual images. For the best results, review the film while you are in a deeply relaxed physical state. It's important that you do no analysis or "study" of the film—simply absorb.

- **Start mentally rehearsing in advance.**

  Get into the regular habit of rehearsing with images how you want to perform and respond during competitive play. This is particularly important with situations that have given you trouble in the past. Set aside regular practice time for your mental rehearsing.

Low Self-Motivation

- **Set meaningful long-term goals.**

  You've got to find a reason to make all the effort and struggle worthwhile. What is your dream as an athlete? Everything begins here.

- **Set realistic intermediate goals.**

  These become the stepping-stones for ultimate success. They must be realistic, challenging, and exciting.

- **Set daily short-term goals.**

Perceived success is the key to self-motivation, and this is how it happens. Success is guaranteed every day when daily short-term goals are properly set.

- **Commit your goals to writing and make a date for completion.**

  The importance of this step cannot be overemphasized. Unless you commit them to paper, the probability of achievement is extremely low.

- **Keep a daily log of your successes.**

  Chart your progress daily. That's what keeps you moving.

- **Associate with highly self-motivated athletes.**

  Motivation is very contagious, both positive and negative. If possible, associate with those who will help you motivationally, not hurt.

- **Make It Fun!**

  Make it fun again. Make that number one in importance. As soon as you are successful, motivational problems will suddenly start evaporating.

Low Positive Energy

- **Joy—Fun—Enthusiasm**

  The energy in its purest form is JOY. It will come when you start thinking and visualizing in the right directions. Competitive sport need not shut off the energy associated with fun, enjoyment, and desire. It too often does, but that can be reversed. The way you construe and picture situations and events in your head makes the difference. Positive energy flow can be rechanneled back into your play by removing the pressure and by seeing things as challenges, rather than as threats.

- **Increase your awareness.**

  Again, awareness is the key to accelerated control. You must learn to recognize when it's flowing and when it's not and what its effects are on your performance.

- **Rehearse energy triggers both on and off the playing field.**

  Certain thoughts and images can become powerful triggers of positive energy. Identify what those are for you, and practice them often. Your "finest hour" as an athlete is often a very powerful one.

- **Do whatever you can to start feeling good about you.**

The better you feel about you, the more positive energy you are likely to have available for sports. Increased self-discipline, better use of your time, and healthier personal relationships are possible examples.
- **High-level physical fitness.**

Exercising right and eating right translates into more physical energy, and that means more mental energy. Poor physical fitness and nutrition directly undermines your efforts to maintain high levels of positive energy.

Low Attitude Control

- **Identify positive and negative attitudes.**

Make a list of the attitudes that hurt you as an athlete and those that help. Try to determine precisely how your negative attitudes get you into trouble.
- **Start repeating to yourself those attitudes that you wish to acquire.**

Attitudes are nothing but habits of thought. The more you start thinking in a particular way, the more likely it is that a habit will develop. This is sometimes called positive affirmation. Throughout the day, you repeat to yourself over and over again those attitudes you wish to develop. They may include such things as, "I'm a positive person," "I'm always going to give 100 percent effort," "I can do it," and "I can control myself."
- **Say "stop."**

Every time a negative thought or attitude surfaces, immediately say "stop" to yourself, and quickly replace it with a positive one.
- **Read, listen, and model.**

Read everything you can that pertains to positive attitudes. Constantly reinforce the right attitudes by reading all the positive thinking books, articles, and magazines that you can. Read the life stories of your heroes in sport. Study their struggles and triumphs.

Whenever possible, listen to audio tapes dealing with positive attitudes and motivation. Many excellent tapes are currently available.

Model the attitudes of champions. Talk to successful athletes whenever you get the chance and ask them about their

attitudes. You will be amazed how quickly you start thinking like a champion when you start acting like one.
* **Keep a record.**
Maintain a daily record of your attitudes. Work hard to be successful with yourself every day.

ADDITIONAL SELF-MONITORING TECHNIQUES

To become the best that you can be requires a special balancing of the mental with the physical. There is such a close connection between our physical bodies and our emotional feeling states that they are often inseparable. We can often control our emotions by controlling the physical body, and conversely, we can often control the physical body by controlling our emotional states, e.g., anger, fear, joy.

Here are 11 areas of training that deal with physical performance factors. Each represents a way to work directly with the physical body to achieve better mental and emotional control.

Eyes

When you are visually focused, you tend to be more mentally and emotionally focused. The more you let your eyes wander during competition, the less likely you will be able to concentrate well. Notice how controlled your eyes are when you're really performing well. Train to keep your eyes always on target during play. In tennis, for example, players should keep their eyes in one of three places between points—on the ball, on the strings, or on the ground. Every sport has different requirements, but the principle is the same—keep your eyes under control at all times.

Rituals

The more ritualistic, the better. Rituals during competition serve to deepen concentration, facilitate muscle relaxation, and help you become more spontaneous. Often our most ritualistic performers are the ones who hold up best under pressure. Rituals help to keep you in rhythm during play and help you to resist the temptation to rush when nervous or angry. Examine your physical rituals. Are they the same each time you step up to shoot a free throw, take a face-off, or execute a three-foot putt? Make sure your rituals are precise, and follow them, most importantly, when you're under pressure and the problems start to mount.

Winning Pace

All great competitors have learned to maintain a special pace during competition. They are able to set the optimum pace for their own best performance and maintain it regardless of the score or existing circumstances. Less successful competitors find their pace constantly changing, often reflecting their emotional state at the time. When they are winning and feel emotionally strong, their pace is excellent; when they are nervous or angry, their pace becomes too fast; when they are losing and feeling low, their pace drags. Train to know your best pace, and keep it at all times, especially under adverse conditions.

Breathing

As discussed in Chapter IV, breathing is a window to your emotions. As we experience different states of feeling (anger, fear, boredom, sadness, excitement, joy), our breathing patterns change. One effective way to control feeling states is to simply take control of your breathing. During competition, monitor your breathing and insure you're sustaining the proper breath pattern and rhythm. Know how you breathe when you are playing great and your IPS is flowing. Again, you need it most when things get difficult.

Project High Positive Intensity

One of the best ways to start feeling high intensity during competition is to project it on the outside with your physical body. If you look "pumped" on the outside, you'll start feeling "pumped" on the inside. You can project intensity with your feet, eyes, face, head, and shoulders. If you want to feel it and can't seem to get it going, FAKE IT! That's often the trigger that makes it happen.

Project Relaxation and Calmness

Every great competitor projects a distinct image of being relaxed and calm in crisis. If you look frantic and tight, you probably are. Work to look more relaxed and calm on the outside. Project an air of no pressure and of being in control. If you can fool those around you into believing you are calm and cool, you're well on your way to being there.

Management of Mistakes

Even when you are performing exceptionally well, you're still making mistakes! We rarely log a perfect performance. When we are performing well, however, we react to mistakes quite differently than when we're performing poorly. When performing well, we go forward as if nothing occurred. We go on with what we're doing and don't get emotionally hung up with the mistake. When playing poorly, however, we respond with negative emotions. Your task, then, is to manage mistakes during competition the way you do when you're performing well.

Project Confident Fighter Image

When the world turns against you, when you're feeling weak, lacking confidence, or when you feel like a wimp—FAKE IT! Project the image of a champion no matter what. Start looking like a confident fighter and you'll soon start feeling like one. Your head, shoulders, and walk must be trained to project confidence.

Negative Self-Talk

The more negative self-talk you get going during competition, the less likely you are to perform well. Negative self-talk stimulates your negative emotions and brings negative energy problems. You can't always stop a negative thought from occurring but you can always stop your negative self-talk. *Keep your self-talk to a minimum* during competition; when it does occur, make it brief and make it positive.

Project a Positive Attitude

When you have trouble controlling your negative thinking, work with your physical body. Project the outward image of someone who is thinking positively and enthusiastically. Look like a positive thinker no matter what.

Project "I Love the Battle"

If you can only project that you love what you are doing when you are winning, you have a long way to go. Train to project the "I love the battle" image at all times, most importantly in crisis.

The following post-competition self-monitoring form should be used to chart your progress over time. Fill it out following competition, as soon as your mind is clear.

Post-Competition Self-Monitoring Form
(Critical Physical Performance Factors)

During Play	Excellent				Poor
1. Eyes Controlled	1	2	3	4	5
2. Rituals	1	2	3	4	5
3. Winning Pace	1	2	3	4	5
4. Breathing	1	2	3	4	5
5. Projected High Positive Intensity	1	2	3	4	5
6. Projected Relaxation and Calmness	1	2	3	4	5
7. Management of Mistakes	1	2	3	4	5
8. Projected Confident Fighter Image	1	2	3	4	5
9. Negative Self-Talk	1	2	3	4	5
10. Projected Positive Attitude	1	2	3	4	5
11. Projected "I Love the Battle"	1	2	3	4	5

Understand What Affects Your Emotions

We've learned the hard way that control of your IPS during competition can be affected by any number of seemingly unrelated factors. The chart on page 186 lists such factors. On this chart, record how much time each day you spend in mental practice, physical practice, stretching, endurance, and speed work. Monitor these activities and determine how they affect your moodiness, confidence, IPS control, and so forth. Research shows that these and such factors as sleep patterns (8 to 9 hours generally optimum), diet, number of meals (4 to 6 small meals generally optimum), and amount of sugar (the less the better) can dramatically affect mood control. Your job is to find out. Determine if you feel more confident when you get your weight on target or when you get better organized throughout the day. If you're a student, how does doing your homework regularly affect how you feel about yourself? Grade yourself A through F on each of the factors as listed in the chart.

Your goal is to fine tune emotionally. For too many athletes, IPS control is out of the question when ideal sleep patterns aren't followed, when diet is poor, or when blood sugar levels are seriously altered by ingesting excessive sugar. Use the chart to understand your moods better. Look for patterns over a six- to eight- week period. Once you know what leads to what, establish your training regime and STAY WITH IT!

MENTAL TOUGHNESS FORMULA

Mental toughness demands control, but there are many things that occur during competition that are beyond your control. We cannot control the wind, cheating opponents, bad refereeing, the condition of the field, fan reaction, and so on. The question is, "How can we stay in control when we are constantly confronted by things beyond our control?"

The answer is at the heart of the Athletic Excellence Training system. Many things do occur that are outside of our control, but we stay *ultimately* in control by CONTROLLING OUR EMOTIONAL RESPONSE TO THOSE EVENTS. I can't control the wind, but I can control my emotional reaction to the wind, and when I do, in a sense, I control the wind.

Consistent success in competition demands that you control what you can and control your emotional response to those things you can't directly control.

Winning is one of those things you can't directly control. You do, however, have direct control over those things that make winning possible: effort, attitude, fight, determination. By training to control these as well as your emotional reactions to uncontrollable events, *you control the situation rather than the situation CONTROLLING you*. And therein lies the key to being a winner!

The following Mental Toughness formula is predicated on control. In my experience, it is a formula that guarantees success if you can consistently answer "yes" to the following four questions following the day's competition:

1. I gave 100 percent of my best effort throughout the contest regardless of outcome.

   In other words, you didn't play it safe emotionally. You tried your hardest until it was over. In no way can you say, "I could have done better if I would have tried harder."

SAMPLE DAILY MONITORING CHART
(For Mood Control)

	Mon	Tues	Wed	Thur	Fri	Sat	Sun
DATE							
Mental Practice (time)							
Physical Practice (time)							
Stretching (yes/no)							
Endurance Work (time)							
Strength Work (time)							
Speed Work (time)							
Total Hours of Sleep							
Time to Bed/Time Up							
Diet (A–F)							
Number of "Meals"							
Sugar—Number of Times							
Weight Every 7 Days							
How Well-Organized (A–F)							
Number of Glasses of Water							
Total Time on Homework							
Mood Control (A–F)							
Off Playing Field (A–F)							
During Play (A–F)							
Positive Intensity (A–F)							
Positive Attitude (A–F)							
Confident Fighter Image (A–F)							
Management of Mistakes (A–F)							
Concentration (A–F)							
Confidence (A–F)							
Motivation (A–F)							
Had Fun (A–F)							
IPS Control (A–F)							
How Well I Played (A–F)							

Other Things Affecting My Mood Today

1.
2.
3.
4.
5.

You put yourself on the line and risked losing, giving your absolute best effort.

2. I kept my energy and attitude positive during the competition, most importantly, during crisis and adversity.

   You didn't turn negative and sour as the problems mounted. If your attitude was to get challenged, inspired, and more determined in response to the problems, you are fast developing the mental toughness skills of a champion.

3. I projected a strong and powerful physical presence during the competition, most importantly during crisis.

   You looked like a winner regardless of the score. You projected the image of a confident fighter throughout the battle. You looked the way you wanted to feel.

4. I offered no excuses!

   You never used a problem as an excuse. You were totally responsible.

If you can answer "yes" to these four statements following the competition, regardless of the score, you were a success. You are, most certainly, winning the mental toughness battle.

THE JOURNEY HOME

Coming home in sport is becoming the best that you can be. The price you must pay to attain proficiency in competitive sport is high. The time, the money, the personal sacrifices, and *the frustrations* create an impressive challenge of the will. The frustrations, for most, represent the greatest obstacle. Too many athletes each year decide that "the price is not worth the payoff." The disappointments, the blood, sweat, and tears cannot be sufficiently balanced.

Some of the price is inevitable and probably even necessary. Rarely does anything *easy* capture our imagination and interest for any length of time. It's the challenge that captures us and the challenge that defeats us. It's the mastery of something that at times seems to approach the realm of the *impossible*. Before long, every new player of the game begins to recognize, "There's more to playing this crazy sport than learning the physical skills." That same message will continue to reverberate in the mind of every dedicated athlete for as long as he or she continues to strive for mastery.

The challenge will *always* be the same. It's an interesting self-discovery when you realize that you never "arrive" as a competitive athlete. You're always "in transit." You're always journeying to somewhere beyond where you are now. Just about the time you think you're about to "arrive," you are shocked with the realization, "I'm barely halfway there." As we more clearly come to understand that the mastery of competitive sport is a process, not a product, the sooner we can flow with the process rather than constantly fight it.

What is the process? It is having it . . . and then losing it. It is struggle. It is discovery. It is failure and defeat, and it is victory. It is going *forward* in all directions—backward, sideways, and upside-down. In a word, it is *TRANSFORMATION*.

The mastery of competitive sport is a process of transformation, of change, of continuous rebirth. The only losers are those who fight the *PROCESS*. The struggle in rebirth is transforming. Don't fight it. Become part of it. Your level of fulfillment and accomplishment will be directly proportionate to your success in going *with* the process rather than *against* it.

Only then will the "price be right." The payoff is the process, and the product is *self-transformation*.

Nowhere is the body-mind connection more delicately balanced than within the arena of competitive sport. Calmness, positive energy, joy, confidence, focus, and positive attitudes are for what, you say? The answer is transformation, transformation leading to *CONTROL*—control of the body-mind connection. This control allows us to extend beyond our ordinary limits, to increase our degree of freedom, and to become a fuller measure of our human potential than thought possible.

Only this transformation can bring us to the very edge of our potential, to our own *limits*. In your quest to "become your ultimate," you will one day fully recognize that *the goal* is not to conquer your noble opponent or the external world, but rather, the conquering of YOURSELF. The opponent and the challenges of the external world are simply vehicles for extending further toward those ultimate limits. They are simply part of the transformation process.

And coming home makes the payoff worth the price.

T. S. Eliot perhaps captured it best when he said:

> *"We shall not cease from exploration,*
> *and the end of our exploring*

Coming home in competitive sport is becoming the best you can be. The process is an experience in self-transformation, and the key to staying on the path is ENJOYMENT. In the final analysis, it becomes a matter of choice.

will be to arrive at the beginning
and know that place for the first
time."

Good Luck on Your Journey . . .

"In searching for the 'sound' of sport, one quickly hears
the roar of the crowd, the crack of the bat and the
thundering of racing feet. But if one listens a little harder
and a little longer, one comes to hear silence. There is
silence within the performer, in the tenseness of the
crowd, in the fear of the hunter and in the beauty of the ski
slopes. Man soon learns that silence is an integral part of
life and that certainly it is prominent in sport. Silence is not
simply the absence of sounds. Rather it is presence. It is
the presence of the dimension of time. A realization of the
instant and the situation."[3]

REFERENCE NOTES

1. Lipsyte, Robert. *Sportsworld* (New York, Quadrangle/New York Times Book Co., 1975), p. 280.
2. Tohei, Koichi. *Ki in Daily Life* (Tokyo: Ki No Kenkyukai H.Q., 1980), p. 22.
3. Slusher, Howard. *Man, Sport and Existence* (Philadelphia, PA: Lea and Febiger, 1967), p. 168.

RECOMMENDED READINGS

Gallwey, Timothy. *The Inner Game of Tennis*. New York: Random House, 1974.

Garfield, Charles A. *Peak Performance*. Jeremy P. Tarcher, Inc., 1984.

Gauron, Eugene. *Mental Training for Peak Performance*. Sport Science Association, 1984.

Herrigel, Eugen. *Zen in the Art of Archery*. New York: Pantheon, 1953.

Kauss, David. *Peak Performance*. New Jersey: Prentice-Hall, 1980.

Klavora, Peter, and Daniel, Juri. *Coach, Athlete, and the Sport Psychologist*. Illinois: Human Kinetics, 1979.

Leonard, George. *The Ultimate Athlete*. New York: Viking, 1975.

Maltz, Maxwell, *Psychocybernetics*. New York: Simon and Schuster, 1960.

McCluggage, Denise. *The Centered Skier*. New York: Warner Books, 1977.

Murphy, Michael, and White, Thea. *The Psychic Side of Sports*. MA: Addison-Wesley, 1978

Nideffer, Robert M. *The Inner Athlete*. New York: Crowell, 1976.

Oates, Bob. *The Winner's Edge*. New York: Mayflower Books, 1980.

Orlick, Terry. *In Pursuit of Excellence*. Illinois: Human Kinetics, 1980.

Ostrander, Sheila, and Schroeder, Lynn. *Superlearning*. New York: Delta, 1979.

Tohei, Koichi. *Ki in Daily Life*. Tokyo: Ki No Kenkyukai H.Q., 1980.